The Story of the
Real Bulldog

by Robert Jenkins and Ken Mollett
TS-290

Dedication

This book is dedicated to the wives and children of the authors, without whose support, input and generosity it could not have been written nor the breeding program accomplished.

"When the stars threw down their spears
And water'd Heaven with their tears:
Did he smile, his work to see?
Did he who made the lamb make thee?"

William Blake (The Tyger)

Distributed in the UNITED STATES to the Pet Trade by T.F.H. Publications, Inc., One T.F.H. Plaza, Neptune City, NJ 07753; distributed in the UNITED STATES to the Bookstore and Library Trade by National Book Network, Inc. 4720 Boston Way, Lanham MD 20706; in CANADA to the Pet Trade by H & L Pet Supplies Inc., 27 Kingston Crescent, Kitchener, Ontario N2B 2T6; Rolf C. Hagen Inc., 3225 Sartelon St. Laurent-Montreal Quebec H4R 1E8; in CANADA to the Book Trade by Vanwell Publishing Ltd., 1 Northrup Crescent, St. Catharines, Ontario L2M 6P5 ; in ENGLAND by T.F.H. Publications, PO Box 15, Waterlooville PO7 6BQ; in AUSTRALIA AND THE SOUTH PACIFIC by T.F.H. (Australia), Pty. Ltd., Box 149, Brookvale 2100 N.S.W., Australia; in NEW ZEALAND by Brooklands Aquarium Ltd. 5 McGiven Drive, New Plymouth, RD1 New Zealand; in Japan by T.F.H. Publications, Japan—Jiro Tsuda, 10-12-3 Ohjidai, Sakura, Chiba 285, Japan; in SOUTH AFRICA by Lopis (Pty) Ltd., P.O. Box 39127, Booysens, 2016, Johannesburg, South Africa. Published by T.F.H. Publications, Inc.
MANUFACTURED IN THE
UNITED STATES OF AMERICA
BY T.F.H. PUBLICATIONS, INC.

Contents

The Dogo Argentino, a bull-breed, was Argentina's first native purebred dog. Photo by Isabelle Francais.

Prologue

One of the purposes of this book is to introduce the reader to "alternative" Bulldogs, especially those called *Victorian*. It has been written for many reasons, not the least of which are to claim for the breeders of these dogs their rightful place in the vanguard of canine development and to dispel any misunderstanding of the breed.

The modern Bulldog is a proud and noble animal, but through the short-sightedness and ignorance of some breeders and show judges, it has been disfigured and distorted. Today, all too often, a modern kennel-club-registered Bulldog carries a list of health problems that any honest veterinarian would denounce as unacceptable.

The decision to remake the breed, for remaking is what has been accomplished, was taken on by various breeders independently of and unknown to each other. This is the story of all those who are trying and succeeding against all odds to give the Bulldog back its dignity and the world back its most noble dog.

There has been and continues to be opposition to their task. Some established breeders of modern kennel-club-registered Bulldogs have called alternative Bulldogs "mongrels" and questioned the motives of their breeders. They have denied the breed entry into their circles. They have questioned, without grounds, the temperament of the dogs and cast aspersions on the nature of those who have tried so hard and for so long to do an honest service to animals. The evidence in this book will answer the doubters and silence the critics.

In any scientific experiment the results must speak
for themselves, and all that breeders of alternative
Bulldogs ask is that you apply the same criteria to their
dogs. Stand them beside modern Bulldogs and see how
much more "Bulldog" they are. Give them a job to do,
and see how well they do it. Take them for a walk, and
see how much fitter and healthier they are. Breed
them, and see how they self-whelp. Own them and see
how well they serve their friends. In short, see how the
Bulldog of a century ago has come home.

In conventional terms the alternative Bulldog may
not be a pedigree animal, but it is not a mongrel. It is
not in the show ring because those in power in the
field of pedigree dogs have shut it out. In any field of
pursuit those who are most established are able to
select those they allow in. They can and do wield their
power mercilessly in order to maintain their position
of superiority. Those who live by the breeding and
selling of modern Bulldogs are often not willing to
open their doors to people whose dogs are stronger,
healthier, more handsome and more genuine than
their own.

Those breeders of modern Bulldogs who recognize
and admit to the problems faced by their breed seek to
correct the faults by using existing stock, but they are
failing and it is possible that they can only fail. Just as
one cannot build a strong house from rotten timber,
so one cannot breed a strong Bulldog without looking
beyond the strict confines of the breed standard.

The breeders in this book realized that their goals
could not be achieved by remaining in a race where
the rules, by their very nature, prevented success. They
realized when they began to chase the Bulldog dream

Schutzhund-titled Terminator, an American Bulldog bred by Sure Grip Kennels, stands 25 ½ inches tall and weighs in at 94 pounds.

that they may be forever outside the conventional show ring. They knew they risked isolation and ill-regard, but despite this they voluntarily chose to enter the margins of the dog breeding world.

It is not the intention of this book to attack anyone, rather it is a setting out of the facts. The case for the alternative Bulldog needs arguing until there are enough of them on the streets of our cities and towns to make their superiority obvious. This book seeks quite simply to address the balance. Until now all the information and propaganda was in the hands of the established breeders. Now for the first time, the reader can decide which is the true Bulldog and which is so called because a judge in a show ring decrees it. At the end of the day it is the contention of those who have written this book that the *dogs* of whatever breed are more important than kennel clubs.

No doubt some sincere and respectable breeders have been left out of this book and to these the authors apologize.

Three bull-breeds: the Bulldog, the French Bulldog, and the Boxer.

The Rise

It is not the purpose of this brief history to apologize for the brutality of past times. Neither is its purpose to give a complete history of our breed. The intention is to detail, in a concise and simple manner, the essential facts and occurrences that helped form the Bulldog.

Serious students of the breed's history are referred to their local libraries, bookshops and colleges and reminded that as much, if not more, information regarding the Bulldog is to be had in the histories of human social development as is to be had in standard breed guides. The Bulldog's history is inseparable from the history of the English-speaking peoples; sanitize either and the truth is lost. If the history of anything is to be studied, then look hard and read all sides of the story before drawing your own conclusions. Until now, the people responsible for giving the Bulldog its best traits never wrote books. Consequently some of the things presented here in relation to the Bulldog are done so for the first time.

If the history of the Bulldog and its makers is brutal, it is not savage. If their tastes and fancies were different to ours in some things, they were the same in others. Remember, the times that spawned the Bulldog spawned Shakespeare and Marlowe, Shelley and Byron, Milton, Blake and Bacon and Drake and Wren.

ORIGINS

The history of the Bulldog is a long and dark one. Many writers on the subject have worried and fussed over the precise date the breed first came to be mentioned in the written word, frequently centering their research on the exact spelling of the breed's name. To spend time on such matters is to not understand the history of the English language. As a written language "English" was not formalized until the early 18th century, and even highly educated people writing previous to the formalizing of the language changed the way they spelled words over and over, often in the same text. Sometimes they would overelaborate a spelling and sometimes use a virtual shorthand. Language, especially when written, is a magical thing, a conjurer of magic and the supernatural, this is why we "spell" a word. In the spelling, we make magic. In spelling a word it is the overall connotation that counts, not the individual arrangement of letters. This history is concerned mostly with the essence of the Bulldog, for the bulldog is more than just a breed of dog definable by some abstract breed standard. What is most important about the Bulldog is its spirit.

When Roman invaders came to Britain, they were met by a people who owned and bred the fiercest dogs in the known world. The invaders, for whom Britain was the last place on the known earth to fall, were already well acquainted with war dogs and fighting dogs. They pitted animals from other conquered lands against the English dogs and found their own breeds inferior. Even the fierce Mollosian dogs of the ancient Greeks were no match, and the Roman writer who informs us of this, Gatius Falliscus, states that there were two types of British Pugnaces, a large and a small type. He so greatly admired the type matched with bulls that he wrote: *It is almost worthwhile making the journey to those far shores to obtain one of this breed, as the*

A statue immortalizing the history of the Bulldog.

courage and ferocity is unmatched by any other breed.
Another Roman writer, Claudiun, (writing AD 395-404), wrote: *The British dogs can break a Bull's neck with just one bite.* Allowing for poetic license on Claudian's part, it is fair to surmise that these dogs could bring down a bull in a most effective manner. He also wrote of: *...the British Hound that brings the bulls big forehead to the ground.*

A Bulldog commemorates the Nylabone® company—makers of the world's safest and most durable chewing devices. Photo by Fotografie Voets & Van Leeuwen, Holland.

Crib and Rosa (circa 1817)–the standard by which all Bulldogs were judged.

With the evidence of Roman chroniclers, it seems fair to surmise that in pre-Roman Britain the Bulldog, or dog for fighting bulls, was already part of British life. The likelihood is then that the breed came with Phoenician traders to Britain in the sixth century BC and became fixed over the subsequent centuries. It is also known that the early Britons took fierce and formidable dogs into battle with them and that Gauls purchased "Bulldogs" from them to use along with their native breeds as war dogs.

After the Norman Conquest of 1066, the Norman passion for writing and record keeping has given us a clearer picture of dogs in sport. We know that animal baiting was common and much patronized by the new monarchy. In 1209, at Stamford, the Earl of Warren was so pleased to observe the spectacle of butcher's dogs chasing bulls from a meadow to the town, he made a gift of the meadow to the townspeople, on the condition that they supplied bulls for such sport on St. Brice's Day each year.

Exactly what this early dog looked like is not clear, but we do have some idea. It was generally called an "Alaunt," and described as ....*being a fighting dog with light brown eyes, truncated muzzle like a monkey, loose folded*

Danzig bear biter, from Riedinger.

Although it is not known exactly what the early "Bulldog" looked like, there are many renditions of early bull fighting dogs.

skin above the brows and a broad back, posed on tall, muscular legs.

It is not a new theory that since these dogs were almost certainly part of the entourage of Henry II when he married Eleanor of Aquitaine, and therefore took possession of Bordeaux, that the dog now known as the Dogue de Bordeaux is the ancestor of the early English Bulldog. It is a point that may be argued, but the Dogue de Bordeaux certainly fits the description of the Alaunt. What cannot be contested is that the English monarchy ruled Bordeaux for over 250 years, holding court there and partaking of bull and bear baiting.

It seems likely that the dog used for baiting bulls in the early days weighed in at around 100 pounds and was a smaller version of the Alaunt. (Alaunt being a

The dog now known as the Dogue de Bordeaux, shown here, is the ancestor of the early English Bulldog. Photo by Isabelle Francais.

term used to describe three different types of dog: *Alan Gentil, Alan Viature* and *Alan de Boucherie.*) In 1406 Edmond de Langley, Duke of York, wrote in his *Master of Game* extracts that read: *An Alaunt by his very nature holds faster when he bites than can three greyhounds of the best that man can find, and therefore is the best hound to hold and seize all manner of beasts, and keep them fast.* He goes on to say that the butcher's Alaunt is used to: *help bring in the beasts from the country, for if an Ox escapes the hounds would go and take hold until their master had come, and should help him bring it to the town again. These Alaunts cost little to feed as they eat the offal found in Butcher's Row. Also they keep their master's house, they are good at bull baiting, and for hunting wild boar.*

Head study of a Dogue de Bordeaux photographed by Isabelle Francais.

Edmond de Langley was "Master of the Game and Hawks" to Henry IV, and it is known that he translated his treatise from an earlier work written by Count Gaston II de Foix et de Bearn, known as Gaston Phoebus. The Count was a very knowledgeable and skilled hunter said to own 600 dogs, and his *Book of the Chase* (*Livre de Chase*) predated Langley's by about 20 years. However, what is most interesting to us here, is that Langley added the mention of bull baiting, where it did not appear in the original. This indicates that bull baiting had become a particularly British use for these Alaunts.

There are many theories regarding the origin of the name "Alaunt" or "Alan." Some suggest that it comes from the Celtic for stag, thus making the original dog a deerhound. Others suggest that it derives from the warrior tribe of the Caucasus, the Alani. Others still suggest that the name is of Spanish origin and that the Alaunt was descended from the Spanish Mastiff, the "Alano." Geoffrey Chaucer, in his *Knight's Tale* (1390), describes the Alaunt, saying: *Therein is a dog of great size, strength and courage.* We also know that this breed went out to Bordeaux between 1151 and 1411 and to Spain, Majorca and Cuba between 1556 and 1649.

It is from the plaque inscribed "Doque de Burgos Espana" dated 1625, that we see an actual likeness of the Bulldog of the time. Even as late as 1799, a note on hounds states in regard to dog classification that: ...*first, the running hounds, which are used to chase hares, etc., the Greyhounds, the Alaunts, or Bulldogs; these were chiefly used for hunting the wild boar.*

It was Henry VIII who set up the office of "Master of the Royal Game of Bears and Mastyve Dogs" (the term

*John Bull and his Bulldog, published in **Punch Magazine** in 1887.*

"Mastiff" believed to be of Norman origin from Latin "Massivus" had been used in earlier writings, often in conjunction with the Alaunt to describe the same dog), but it was under the patronage of his daughter Queen Elizabeth I (1558-1603) that the sports of bull and bear baiting became most popular. It is said that she so loved the sport that on one visit to the Earl of Leicester, he supplied 13 bears to be baited for her amusement. On May 25, 1559, she gave a dinner party for the French Ambassador following a baiting of bulls and bears, and the next day they enjoyed the entertainment again, this time at St. Paul's Wharf.

There is a map of London, dated 1547, that shows two amphitheaters marked for "The bayting of bowles and bears," and one can only guess at the mortality rate of dogs pitted against such physically superior

The Bulldog's journey to life.

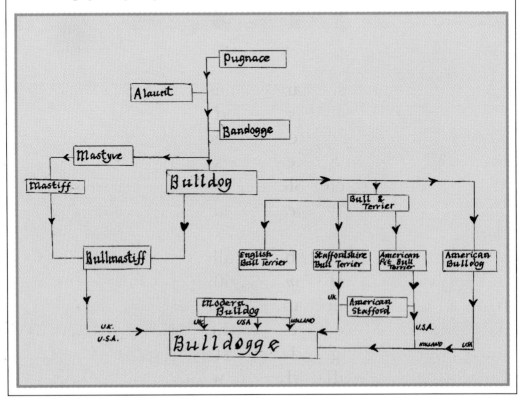

Brabant Bull Biter, from Riedinger.

opponents as bears. Bears such as Sackerson, Harry
Hunks, Tom of Lincoln and Ned of Canterbury
survived dozens of contests to become celebrities in
their own right. In Shakespeare's *Merry Wives of
Windsor*, the character Slender boasts: *I have seen
Sackerson loose twenty times, and have taken him by the
chain...*

Ben Jonson mentions both Bulldogs and "Beardogs"
in his play *The Silent Woman* (1609). But it is in a letter
from an English merchant in Spain, Preston Eastwick,
dated 1631, that we have both the closest proximity to
the modern spelling and the first distinction between
Bulldogs and Mastiffs, when he wrote home for sup-

Le Dogue de Forte Race.

plies and: *...a good mastive dogge...and two good Bulldoggs.*
This correspondence is important because it also
demonstrates that Bulldogs were still being imported
to Spain, a full 70 years after some were imported by
Philip II.

Then in 1707, Guy Miege stated: *Our Mastiffs, especially the ones we call Bulldogs, are of unmatchable courage.
One of these dogs will fight anything alone, bear, tiger, or
lion, and will not quit his hold till he gets the victory or loses
his life.*

It is certain that the Bulldog is an ancient breed
native to the shores of Britain since before written
history, and its development is very much entwined in
the social evolution of England and the English speaking world. But it is more than that. The Bulldog is a
leftover from the days when terms such as chivalry,
honor, courage and decency were not clichés. It is a
leftover from the days when a battle was settled in
close combat, when the leaders of men led from the
front, and when the respect of brothers was more
important than the silver in one's purse.

That a nation or individual when likened to a Bulldog is paid the highest compliment is no accident. A
Bulldog may be trampled, torn apart, crushed, or
gored to death by superior force but the Bulldog dies
facing its opponent unafraid, defeated but not
conquered, bloodied and broken but not bowed. For a
Bulldog to relinquish its grip or attack any part of its
opponent other than the front, square on, would be
unforgivable.

When we look in more detail at the sporting games
that honed our breed to perfection, we must do so not
as moralists and judges of human behavior, but with an

eye on the behavior of the dogs. Just as no one, not even the most extreme animal liberation organization blames the Foxhound for fox hunting or the Otterhound for the demise of the Otter, we must beware of blaming the Bulldog for its own brutal history. We must remember that the Bulldog became so revered because it was not only savage when savagery was warranted, but a gentle, loyal dog at all other times. What the Bulldog is, people made it; and until this century they made it well. Through, and perhaps despite, all the brutality of man, something special was forged.

BULLDOGS IN SPORT

Bull running, confined for the most part to rural areas, features in the history of the Bulldog only as a predecessor of organized "modern" bull baiting. It is probable that its origins lie in sacrificial customs that predate Christianity and it remained as a pastime, perhaps with some superstitious connotations, until its eventual outlawing.

The first bull running to be dealt with as a sport and assigned to written history was in 1209 at Stamford in Lincolnshire, but it is certain that the sport became popular on a much wider front with the passing of time. Such occasions are said to have attracted the "lowest" and most "base" people in their droves, and commentators point out frequently that the events were akin to riots.

The bull was loosed from a darkened stall and goaded into action by groups of men. It was not un-common for an unwilling bull to have its flesh lacerated and spirit poured into the wounds to

An early drawing of the Boxer.

The Bulldog became so revered not only because it was savage when savagery was warranted but also because it was a gentle and loyal dog at all other times.

Danzig Bear Biter, from Flemming.

increase its aggression. Men and dogs would cause the
bull to run furiously through the town, then they
would drive it onto a bridge and heave it into a river,
or perhaps cut pieces of its body from it as it ran in
blind frenzy and pain towards town or county
boundaries.

The sport, though it had rules, it was mostly haphaz-
ard. It was localized and centered for the most part in
the towns of Stamford, Tutbury and Tetbury. Beyond
these places there is little written history to lend us a
more accurate picture, but if we consider the way
sports such as football and rugby came to be
established, we can see that the widespread
disorganized development of pastimes was the norm
throughout the centuries.

It wasn't long, however, before the bull-running
games gave way in popularity to bull baiting, and it is
for this sport that our breed is most famous and gets

its name. In England, as in many parts of Europe during the middle-ages, almost every town and village had a bullring and the sport was popular with every class and social group. Fitz-Stephen, writing in his *Description of the City of London* (1174), informs us that in the morning of every winter holiday young Londoners were entertained by the sight of boars fighting each other or bulls and full grown bears being baited by dogs.

The Bulldog has long been a formidable guardian and protector.

The baiting sports usually took place on a Sunday and were suitable outlets of aggression for a nation used to being at war. Only the Puritans thought the sport wrong, and when scaffolding fell at the Paris-Garden, a famous baiting ring owned and established by Robert de Paris at Bankside in Southwark, London, on 15th January 1583, the Puritans thought it a righteous judgment for baiting on the Lord's day. Unfortunately, not long afterwards, a church roof fell in killing several Puritans at Sunday Service, and a young man is reported as saying that: *It serves them right for being in church when they could have been at a good baiting!*

An early drawing of Bulldog ancestors.

Doctor John Kaye (1510-1573) wrote of the dog used in these contests: *It is the kind of dog capable of courage, violent and valiant, striking cold fear into the hearts of men but standing in fear of no men in so much that no weapons will abridge his boldness.*

In most baitings, the bull was tethered by a long rope or chain, allowing it to turn a full circle within a walled or fenced ring. The dogs were set to it often one at a time, but sometimes in pairs, and if the bait was prolonged, pairs of dogs would be set on the bull in waves. So that as two were killed or pulled out wounded, another two would replace them. John Houghton wrote: *I'll say something of baiting the bull, which is by having a collar about his neck, fastened to a thick rope about three, four, or five yards long, hung to a hook so fastened to a stake that it will turn around. With this the bull circulates to watch his enemy, which is a bull dog (commonly used for this sport), with a short nose that his teeth may take the better hold...*

A short nose also meant that when the full bite was on, the Bulldog's breathing was not affected. It is ironic that the very aspect of the breed that was needed in order to let the dog breathe was accentuated to such a degree in the early 20th century that it had the reverse effect.

Houghton went on: *I believe I have seen dogs tossed 30 if not 40 feet into the air and when they are tossed either*

A Spanish medallion depicting the head of a Bulldog dated 1625.

higher or lower, the men about strive to catch them on their shoulders lest the fall might mischief the dogs. They commonly laid sand about that if they fell it might be easier. Notwithstanding this great care, a great many dogs were killed, more had their limbs broken and some held so fast that by the bull swinging them, their teeth were often broken out. Often the men were tossed as well as the dogs. One bull

An early postcard.

An early postcard. Note the muzzle.

dog being tossed broke a leg in its fall. The leg was instantly spliced and the dog again, in that maimed condition, ran at the bull. Nothing but greater force than is in his power to exert could break the hold of the bulldog and he was endowed by nature with the highest possible degree of courage. The custom was for owners of dogs who wished to bait the bull to each pay entrance fees and if their dog pinned the bull they received a prize. The reward might be five shillings, a gold laced hat, a silver watch or an ornate dog collar. Many great wagers were laid on both sides and great journeys would men and dogs go on for such diversions.

An early business card for a portrait studio. Note the obvious Pug blood.

It should be noted that even granting poetic license to John Houghton, it is unlikely that a very large dog could be tossed so high, let alone be caught on the shoulders of the spectators. It is likely then that the Bulldog of this period didn't weigh much more than around 80 pounds. The dog would need a certain body weight to tire the bull, and great strength in order to hold on. Provided the Bulldog held fast, the bull, in trying to shake him off, would exhaust himself. This exhaustion coupled with loss of blood and sheer terror would be essential to the Bulldog's victory. It is fair to surmise

An early postcard with a fashionable lady of the times.

that the dog would need to be a middle weight and not a full mastiff, nor a light "terrier" type dog. For bull baiting in the middle ages and after, taking place in a fixed arena, a Bulldog would not require the stamina or fleet-footedness of the dogs used in the earlier bull running, and the greater emphasis fell on developing a dog that was less leggy and more powerful.

That these baits were brutal is beyond doubt, but it must be remembered that the Bulldog was as much a victim of this brutality as the bull. Sporting periodicals of the 18th century report that at the baitings owners of bitches with pups for sale would often send their dogs against the bull in order to prove the worth and breeding of the pups. A good

An early postcard.

TRUE TO THE FLAG.

Britons hold your own, *Tennyson.*

ON GUARD !

Old postcards are always a delight, as they show how much the Bulldog has changed.

performance would dramatically increase the value of a litter, and there are records of the men cutting their bitches to pieces once they have a good hold on the bull in order to demonstrate that even faced with such extra savagery they would not relinquish their grip. One man, at regular intervals, cut off his bitches' legs

In baiting, the Bulldog was as much a victim as the bull.

as they held the bull, and afterwards, they hobbled back to him on bloodied stumps while he sliced off their heads. He proved their loyalty and tenacious quality and sold their pups for a better price.

It is a puzzle of human nature that while this kind of brutality abounded in the street, writers, philosophers and scientists were creating masterpieces of culture and pushing back the bounds of knowledge. A public notice of 1721, 11 years after the completion of St. Paul's Cathedral, states: *...note: also a bear to be baited and a mad green bull to be turned loose in the gaming place; with fireworks all over him and a comet at his tail, and Bulldogs after him. A dog will be drawn up with fireworks after him in the middle of the yard.*

The last part of the notice refers to the practice of using a rope and pulley to haul a Bulldog over fire. He kept safe by holding on fast to the end of the ropes.

An early postcard.

Boxing matches mostly between men but often featuring women were common after a baiting contest and it is reported that these combined events attracted up to and in excess of five thousand spectators.

One William Taplin wrote in *The Sportsman's Cabinet: It is a distinguishing and invariable trait in the true-bred Bulldog to attack the animal in front and never to make*

The Bulldog was known as the dog with the short body.

cowardly attempt at the extremities. The dog whose breed has been preserved genuine and incontaminate aims at and makes most ferociously for the face of the bull, and sinking closer to the ground the nearer he approaches, makes a desperate effort to seize upon the lip, failing in which he relaxes not in his efforts but with the most incredible and determined fury fastens upon the tongue, the eyes, the under jaw, the throat, or some part about the head or face (never degrading his character by making a pusillanious attempt behind) where having secured his hold he retains it beyond the power of description in opposition to every energetic and desperate effort of the bull to get himself disengaged from so furious and bloodthirsty an opponent. Taplin goes on to say the Bulldog's hold is beyond the conception of any who have not borne witness to it.

The baiting of the bull ended with either the dog defeated and withdrawn, or the bull submitting to the dog and letting itself be drawn down or around the ring. The bull was then invariably slaughtered and the meat considered more tender.

Frequently the bulls used were not simply farm animals, but as in modern-day bull-fighting, were often "trained" for action. They were often more aggressive than the ordinary bull and would have an idea of what to expect, having met Bulldogs before in practice sessions when the dogs would not have been allowed to go "full in."

It was not until 1802 that the first attempt came before Parliament to have the sport outlawed. During the debate, Lord Sheridan said: *cruelty to the bull is not the only cruelty exercised on these occasions. What sort of moral lesson, for instance, is it to the children of the farmer who brings his aged bull-bitch, many years the faithful sentinel of his house and farmyard, surrounded by her pups to prove at the bull-ring the staunchness of her breed? He brings her forward, sets her at the infuriated animal, she seizes him by the nose and pins him to the ground...but what is the reward from her owner? Applause from the mob for his favourite animal? He calls for a hedging-bill and to prove her breed hews her to pieces without her quitting her grip, while he sells her puppies at five guineas a piece.*

However, it seems that the greatest outcry was not on the grounds of animal welfare, but rather that concern

An early drawing of a Bulldog bitch and her pups.

An early rendition of a Boston Terrier named Bob.

for the bull and dog was a guise behind which religious groups and those of "sensitive dispositions" could launch attacks on the pastimes of working class or poor people.

The Reverend Charles Townsend, a reformer of the times, revealed his true intentions and feelings with this speech: *On the minds of men addicted to them only look around a moment amongst your own acquaintances of this sort. What kind of husbands do they make? Are their wives as cheerful and happy as they have the means of making them? Are their children as well clothed, as well fed, and as well taught as they might be? At the conclusion of a bull baiting where do the principle parties concerned in it most commonly resort? Do they go straight home to their families, or straight away in the Ale House, where gambling, drinking and swearing are the order of the day? Then let me ask, who but a bull-baiter ever turned his own infant out of the cradle to put his crippled dog in its place? Who else robbed his suckling child of the mother's breast that a whelp of a favourite breed might be nourished with the food to which it was considered to have the best title of the two?*

An article in *British Field Sports* (1818) read: *The Bulldog, devoted solely to the most barbarous and infamous purposes. The real blackguard of his species has no claim upon the utility, humanity, or common sense and the total extinction of the breed is a desirable consummation.*

One of Ken Molletts Victorian Bulldogs. Seeing is believing...

An early postcard from Switzerland.

An early postcard depicting the gentleness of the Bulldog.

Despite the strong words, the bill was defeated in Parliament, and bull baiting continued. Another attempt was made in 1829, this time losing by 45 votes, but with mounting pressure and final abandonment of

Throughout the history of the Bulldog, there were many strains of various sizes. This is an early sketch of a small Bulldog.

bull baiting by the higher social classes, a bill against what was termed "This Hellish Pastime" was finally passed in 1835. The banning, however, did not stop the sport entirely and the law was not applied with any real conviction for another 20 years.

One of the most famous breeders of fighting Bulldogs was Ben White, who had his kennels at Old Conduit Field, Bayswater, London, and who advertised: *Dogs kept, broke, chained and cured of most disorders for gentlemen on most reasonable terms. Large accommodation pit for gentlemen to experience the goodness of the dogs previous to purchasing, to fight the badger or one with the other, which they please.*

What is important about Ben White's kennels is that after he moved his business to May Tree Cottage, Kensal Rise, he passed away and his business was purchased by Mr. William George (1805-1991), who renamed the kennels "Canine Castle" and set about breeding the best Bulldogs and Mastiffs money could buy.

This take-over took place three years after the Bulldog was supposedly made redundant by the abolition of baiting.

William George was also one of the people who introduced the Spanish Bulldog or "Perros de Toros" to England. In 1840 he imported a dog from Spain that he named "Big Headed Billy," a brindle pied dog of some 90 pounds and apparently the same type depicted on the plaque at Burgos in 1625.

It is quite possible that William George was simply bringing back one of the descendants of the Bulldogs exported to Spain in the preceding centuries, and if so, the dog would have been of British, or part British, blood. What is without question is that William (Bill) George built a world-wide reputation for breeding fine dogs and was visited by Charles Dickens on more than one occasion, as well as featured in books by his contemporaries and in magazines like "Punch." Captain Garnier, a renowned breeder of Mastiffs, said of "Bill" George: *I bought of him a pair of Mastiffs whose produce by goodluck afterwards turned out some of the finest specimens of the breed I ever saw.*

But it is undeniable that with the outlawing of the sport the Bulldog was deliberately evolved to engage in, a darkness appeared on the horizon. Once a working dog has no work to do, it risks becoming a fashion accessory.

Although bull baiting had the longest run of the popular baiting sports, nothing in England, except perhaps hating the French, was as popular as bear baiting during its heyday. From around 1550 through the late sixteen hundreds bear baiting left all other pastimes in its wake. Supported by the Court and Aristocracy, the Bear Gardens were the most patronized of all baiting establishments.

Perros de Toros Anno, 1853.

Bears being more expensive than bulls, and harder to come by, were often supplied by the higher classes for the contests. No-one, but no-one, was above partaking in this sport. From the Monarch to Sir Walter Raleigh, to the apprentices and tradesmen, to the ruffians and harlots, all enjoyed bear baiting.

It was common to take visiting Ambassadors from far-flung countries to see a display of Bulldog on bear, and all the visiting dignitaries were of the opinion that they had nothing in their native lands to compare. This may have been good diplomacy and self

A Bulldog used in war propaganda.

preservation, but was also probably true. That bear baiting hit a high note after 1650 should not blind us to the fact that it had certainly been popular long before, and quite possibly even prior to, the Roman invasion.

The bears themselves, if proven capable and eager fighters, became celebrities. Some survived many contests and killed many dogs. They were aided in this

The Bulldog was often the victim of human abuse.

"INVINCIBLE"

TALBOT

The "R.A." of BRITISH CARS

Specifications and full particulars on request.

CLEMENT TALBOT, Ltd. (Dep. C 5), Automobile Engineers, Barlby Road, Ladbroke Grove,
LONDON, W.

Telegrams: "Clemtal, London."   Telephone: 5006 Paddington.

Healthy Bulldogs were often used in advertising to depict strength and endurance.

by virtue of being tethered to a chain by a metal collar, the collar providing protection for the throat. If a bear repeatedly did well, and the odds were too much in its favor, it might have the collar removed. When this occurred, the tables invariably turned the Bulldog's way and the bear was killed. It was also known for "white" or "Polar" bears to be released into the Thames and the Bulldogs to bait the animals while swimming.

Whatever the outcome of any match, one can only be in awe of the courage of the dogs who, weighing between 50 and 100 pounds, were wiling to engage in combat with creatures of such vast physical superiority. That the Bulldog frequently won is incredible.

As the centuries progressed, the pastime eventually slipped from fashion with the higher classes and became a sport solely for the poor, until its final abolition along with bull baiting in 1835.

As well as the aforementioned games, Bulldogs were used sporadically against lions and monkeys too. Once again we are faced with the probability that dogs were pitched against lions at a very early date. We know that Mastiffs were used in Roman arenas against lions, Christians and gladiators, and the fact is that the spectacle of lion baiting probably predates Roman times quite considerably.

However, for our purposes the first record of a Bulldog against lions occurred during the reign of James I (1603-1625). Apparently he ordered the three best Mastiffs to be brought to Paris-Garden in London and set upon a lion one by one. The third and only surviving dog bit so hard and held so well that the lion retired to its den, licking its wounds. Whereupon King

James I ordered this courageous dog never to be pitted again but to be well looked after. At the time of this bait, the difference between Bulldogs and Mastiffs was only just becoming distinct, and many commentators used the breed names to describe what was, to all intents and purposes, the same dog. At the same time, Mastiffs and Bulldogs were sometimes called Bandogges or Bondogges. This derived from the fact that in order to protect the innocent, and to ensure the dogs only came to grips with a legitimate target, often these dogs were kept chained. A chain in old English being the vulgar of the Saxon "Banda."

The special baiting enjoyed by James I was organized by Edward Alleyn, better known as an actor and producer of plays, as a keeper of brothels and also as the philanthropic founder of Dulwich College. In 1604 Edward Alleyn and his father-in-law purchased the Court office of "Chief Master, Ruler and Overseer of All and Singular Games of Bears and Bulls and Mastiff dogs and Mastiff Bitches." This title gave them the Royal authority to use any Mastiffs they chose, with or without the owner's consent, for the sport of baiting. It is mostly from this office, and from ensuring the public got what it wanted, that Alleyn amassed his fortune.

The use of Bulldogs against lions continued for over two hundred years, although on a much smaller scale than the baiting of other beasts. Even in 1825, lions were baited against Bulldogs in Warwickshire. On this occasion the victory was with the lion. Again, however, it is the courage of the dog that stands as the most remarkable feature of the event and not the result.

Tigers were occasionally baited, and there is one record of such an animal being baited to death. There are enough historical references for us to conclude that one on one, a Bulldog is no match for a lion or tiger (as if we didn't know that already). However, used as a team of three, four or five, Bulldogs could win the day over any beast ever brought to the baiting ring.

Against monkeys the Bulldog again had a good record, though these contests only really took place

In the days of bull baiting, the Bulldog's short nose allowed his breathing to remain unaffected when he had a full bite on the bull.

between 1799 and 1822 and mostly involved "Bulldog cross Terriers" or Bull Terriers. Neither were they baits as such, but straight one on one fights. As a rule, if the monkey was unarmed, the Bulldog won; but if the monkey was allowed to wield a club, victory most frequently went the other way.

With the demise of baiting, only dog fighting remained as a sport the Bulldog could shine in, and here it was thought a lighter, faster animal was more likely

to do well. The crossing of Bulldogs and Terriers increased, bringing us the modern day Bull Terrier and
the Staffordshire Bull Terrier, and the Bulldog became
at risk of complete extinction.

It is thanks to dedicated fanciers in the communities
of the lower classes that the Bulldog survived at all, and
our gratitude to these people cannot be too great.
Those few people remembered the dogs and their
history and banded together to begin the showing of
specimens in public houses. It is from these shows that
dog showing as we know it today evolved, and against
the propaganda of the higher classes, the Bulldog
people stood firm. To appreciate the weight of feeling
against the Bulldog at the time, it is worth recalling the
quote from *British Field Sports* (1818): *The Bulldog,
devoted solely to the most barbarous and infamous purposes.
The real blackguard of his species has no claim upon the*

American Pit Bull Terrier photographed by Isabelle Francais.

Staffordshire Bull Terrier photographed by Isabelle Francais.

utility, humanity, or common sense and the total extinction of the breed is a desirable consummation.

The Bulldog in bloody sport was finished but the Bulldog itself was not, and neither was Man's brutality and abuse of the breed.

Mr. Vero Shaw's Bulldogs, Smasher and Sugar.

An early postcard.

The Fall

The working men who showed their Bulldogs would meet in ale houses, chip in money for a fancy collar or some other token trophy, and show their animals for the honor of the trivial prize. More often than not the shows took place on sawdust-covered floors in the big cities and were popular with men who fought dogs too. There was no loss of face in the Bulldog becoming a show animal, and some that were shown were also used in pits.

The "type" for the perfect Bulldog was widely recognized as being "Rosa" and "Crib," and it was on these dogs that the Bulldog standard was set. However, it was also at around this time that some fanciers of the breed decided to "bantamize" their animals. The process of miniaturization happened over a period of about ten years and involved crossing the Bulldog with the Pug, the average weight of which was 20 pounds. By using only the smallest and lightest pups in each litter, they eventually produced dogs weighing as little as 12 pounds. Many of these small animals were exported to France and probably formed the foundation for the French Bulldog, although most modern breeders of French Bulldogs will not entertain the idea.

Despite the crossing of the Bulldog with other breeds to satisfy the movement of fashion in the show ring, there were many breeders who swore by the superiority of the pure-bred Bulldog, especially in a fight to the death, and refused to cross their animals with another breed. Even though it is doubtful whether any pure-bred Bulldogs fought in the pit after 1840, when the faster Bull Terrier was proving its worth, the champions of the "working" Bulldog kept faith with the breed.

Around this time in a book by J.H. Walsh, *The Dog in Health and Disease*, the Bulldog is described under the heading of "Watch Dogs and House Dogs" and the passage is reprinted here in full:

F. Cuvier has asserted that this dog has a brain smaller than any other of his congeners, and in this way accounts for his assumed want of sagacity. But though this authority is deservedly high, I must beg leave to doubt the fact as well as the inference; for if the brain is weighed with the body of the dog from which it was taken it will be found to be relatively about the average, the mistake arising from the evident dis-proportion between the brain and the skull. The whole head,

Mr. Shirley's Kennels at Newbold, Warwickshire, circa 1886.

Mr. Meager's Bulldog Bismarck.

including the zygomatic arches and cheek bones, is so much larger than that of the spaniel of the same total weight of body that the brain may well look small, as it lies in the middle of the various processes intended for the attachment of the strong muscles of the jaw and neck.

I was able to obtain the fresh brain of a pure Bulldog for the purpose of comparison in 1879, and from examination I have no doubt of the fact being as above stated. The mental qualities of the Bulldog may be highly cultivated and in brute courage and unyielding tenacity of purpose he stands unrivalled among quadrupeds, and with the single exception of the game-cock he has no parallel in these respects in the brute creation.

Two remarkable features are met with in this breed. Firstly, they always make their attack at the head; and secondly, they do not bite and let go their hold, but retain it in the most tenacious manner, so that they can with difficulty be removed by any force which can be applied. Instances have been recorded in which Bulldogs have hung on to the lip of the bull (in the old days of baiting that animal) after their entrails have been torn out, and whilst they are in the last agonies of death. In this way they are assisted by the shortness of the face which allows the nostrils to remain potent, even when the nose and mouth are embedded in any soft substance.

Indeed when they do lay hold of an object, it is always necessary to choke them off, without which resource they would scarcely ever be persuaded to let go.

An early drawing of a Greyhound and a Bulldog.

Two early Bulldogs, Bully II and Dorinda.

From confinement in their kennels they are often deficient in intelligence, and they can rarely be brought under good control by education; and from the same circumstance they show little personal attachment, so that they are almost as likely to attack their friends as their enemies in their fury when their blood is up.

Many a Bulldog has pinned his master's leg in revenge for a tread on his foot and it is very seldom that liberties can be taken with him by anyone.

There is an old story strongly characteristic of this tendency, which will illustrate this passion for pinning and also the fondness of the lower orders in some districts from the fighting and baiting propensities of their dogs. A Staffordshire coal-miner was one day playing with his Bulldog, an unentered puppy, when the animal became angry and pinned his master by the nose. On this the bystanders became alarmed and were going to treat the dog roughly but the owner interfered with, "don't touch us, Bull: let un *taste blood, an' it'll be the meaking on him." And so the puppy was allowed to hang on and worry his master's nose to his heart's content.*

Most writers, whether political or otherwise, are fond of dilating on the "Bulldog courage" of Englishmen, yet in the same breath they vilely asperse the noble animal from whom they draw their simile. The Bulldog has been described as stupidly ferocious, and showing little preference for his master over strangers; but this is untrue, he being an excellent watch, and as a guard unequalled, except perhaps by the Bull-mastiff a direct cross from him. Indeed he is far from being quarrelsome by nature, though the Bull-Terrier in many cases undoubtedly is so, and I fancy that some writers have taken their description from this dog rather than the pure Bulldog, which has been at all times rather a scarce animal.

A print by Louis Wain, circa 1894, depicting early Bulldogs and Poodles.

An early Bulldog, Exodus.

If once the pure breed is allowed to drop, the best means of infusing fresh courage into degenerate strains will be finally lost, except for the addition of extraneous blood, which may not suit them; for I believe that every kind of dog possessed of very high courage owes it to a cross with the Bulldog; and thus the most plucky greyhounds, foxhounds, mastiffs, pointers, etc. may all be traced to this source. Though bull and badger baiting may not be capable of extenuation, to them we

An early sketch of a Bulldog.

owe the keeping up of this breed in all its purity; and though we may agree to discontinue those old fashioned sports, yet I am sure my brother sportsmen will see the bad taste of running down a dog who, with all his faults, is not only the most courageous dog, but the most courageous animal in the world.

An attempt has recently been made by Mr. Adcock, who is a most enthusiastic lover and breeder of the Bulldog, to show that he was originally much larger than the English Bulldog of the first half of the present century. My own opinion is, that he has altogether failed, and that, instead of 70 or 80 lb., which is the weight he insists on, 45 to 50 lb. should be considered correct. The Bulldog Club have arrived at the same conclusion and have recorded their opinion in a scale of points.

It would appear from the last paragraph that the Bulldog weighs progressively less throughout its development from early recorded times until the final abolition of bull baiting. Without awakening the sport of bull baiting in order to see first hand which dogs do well and which don't, we shall never know quite why the breeders whose dogs were set to the bull bred down in size. But it was obviously a conscious and deliberate act.

However, like all things there were several different camps and opinions, and highly knowledgeable people held conflicting opinions on the ideal size of the dog. Many breeds that are part Bulldog in their foundation set no upper limit for size and weight, provided proportion is present, and it is quite likely that throughout the history of the Bulldog, there were many strains of various sizes.

Breeding dogs is not and never can be an exact science, and type changes as size does. What breeders do is match two good but imperfect examples in search of a better one. Each breeder will have a personal idea of the best weight, shape and look, and it was always this way.

The mention in the above quote of Mr. Adcock being a supporter of the larger type of Bulldog brings us back to the Spanish Bulldog. We know that Bill George imported a Bulldog from Spain, "Big Headed Billy," in 1840 and set about breeding with him. However, the only available evidence of Bill George actually showing a dog was at an early show in 1862. He came in second with a white dog, "Big Headed Dan," a grandson of "Big Headed Billy." Where "Billy" weighed in at 90 pounds, his grandson "Dan" was only 65 pounds. "Big Headed Dan" was obviously a good Bulldog because a gentleman bought him from Bill George for the then princely sum of 100 pounds (his new owner apparently taking "Dan" along to a hotel where he proudly performed his party piece of jumping through a glass window and emerging unscathed).

The Spanish Bulldog is a lot less foreign than might at first be supposed and it is fair to assume that this blood entered the Bulldog through Bill George's efforts. He was a breeder of distinction and would not have gone to such efforts for no reason, so we can also assume that the Bulldog benefited by his breeding program.

In 1868 a Mr. Marquart imported two more Spanish Bulldogs (Bon Homme and Lisbon) and five years later, in 1873, Mr. Frank Adcock (as mentioned in the book by J.H. Walsh) brought over two more (Toro and Alphonse). All these dogs weighed around 90 pounds. Toro stood 22 inches at the shoulder with a 22-inch

An early sketch of the original bull and terrier cross, circa 1890.

circumference skull and measured 2 $^1/_2$ inches from the corner of the eye to the tip of the nose. They were all reported to be exceedingly muscular and active. They had deep flews, large nostrils, a deep stop, were moderately short in the face and considerably undershot. They were very wrinkled, had a deep, double dewlap, thick and muscular neck, muscular shoulders, large feet, broad and deep chest and round ribs. There was considerable fall at the shoulders, and from that point the loins began to rise. The hindquarters were small compared with the forequarters and considerably higher. All had close cropped ears.

It appears that Mr. Frank Adcock was an enthusiastic Bulldog lover who regularly showed his dogs, seemingly winning with some of Bill George's breeding and sparking a power struggle within the Bulldog circles. Many of Adcock's contemporaries didn't consider the Spanish bloodlines pure enough, and it is quite likely that this struggle resulted in the founding of the Bulldog Club in 1875. Although the accepted standard was modeled on Crib and Rosa and the engraving of them was considered to depict perfection in a Bulldog, they were soon knocked from their pedestal by the shorter, cobbier dogs that were becoming the fashion.

The Spanish Bulldogs were no longer shown but they were used at stud by some fanciers. In 1895, two prominent men in Bulldog circles, Sam Woodiwiss, Judge and Vice-president of the Bulldog Club, and Mr. H.C. Brook, Secretary of the South London Bulldog Club, imported Dogues de Bordeaux, but edicts of the Kennel Club in 1898 forbid them in the show ring and ended their usefulness in England.

There is no solid proof that after the Spanish dogs the Bulldog was ever crossed with another breed, although there were frequent whispers about breeders using Bullmastiff bitches to add size and substance to their line where it had been lost in the bantamizing of earlier years. Whether there was any truth in the whispers is unknown, but certainly some Bulldogs were

An early photograph pays tribute to the Boxer, circa 1906.

again coming in at over 70 pounds, although, better rearing of pups must also have contributed to the increase in weight.

As early as 1896 there were backlashes against the way Bulldog breeding and showing was going. With no work to do, the Bulldog was at the mercy of every judge's whim and fancy, and a group of old-type Bulldog lovers got together to hold an alternative show. Their show, at the Blue Anchor Public House in Shoreditch, London, was not recognized by the Kennel Club or the Bulldog Club but attracted an entrance of 35 dogs and many spectators.

Sadly, the alternative breeders and showers were swept away by fashion. As the 20th century opened, it saw an increase in Bulldog breeding activity and total ignorance on the part of the breeders and judges regarding the Bulldog as it was supposed to be.

It would seem that one of the biggest errors of the Bulldog fancy was the following of Jacob Lamphiers "Properties and Points of the Bulldog." It is item Number 5 which would seem to be responsible for so many wrongs against the breed, it reads: *The face (1) Shortness: Measured from the front of cheekbone to the end of the nose: THIS POINT CANNOT BE CARRIED TO GREAT AN EXCESS.* The embracing of this guide by judges and breeders, probably more than any other single event, damaged the Bulldog's health, and it is between the two World Wars and after that the greatest mistakes were made.

In recent times a survey was carried out of the birth of Bulldog litters and found that of over 150 litters observed, only 6% were "natural whelpers." The necessity of cesarean section deliveries is accepted by many breeders as a fact of life, and little is done to improve the inherited defects that breeding for fashion has caused.

One of the most prominent breeders of the inter-war years was Captain Berger-Wheeler, who bred some magnificent Bulldogs and is recorded as saying: *I have from time to time to criticize certain post-war tendencies, and to deplore the shapeless and badly balanced bodies that are all too common.* When praising a dog he admired he went on to say: *I was shattered with the remark that he was much too long on the leg. This gave me a clue to the ideas of the younger generation and led me to understand how some of them are going after false gods.*

An early sketch of the Bulldog. Note the chain. Bulldogs used for baiting were often confined to kennels rather than kept in the house.

At some point in the history of the Bulldog, power moved from those who wanted a powerful working animal to those who wanted a toy or companion. Unfortunately, unlike with most other breeds where this happened, those who wanted the toy were unwilling to entertain the aspirations of the breeders who wanted the more agile, fitter animal. The insistence of those in power was that only one "Bulldog" was in existence, and ultimately the breed was corrupted by such self-protecting lack of vision. History books were reinterpreted and re-written in order that the new power holders seemed just and right, and the modern kennel-club-registered Bulldog took shape.

There must have been many dissenters and many broken-hearted breeders who showing their dog perhaps a Bulldog of exemplary quality and breeding, lost out to the type most popular with the fashion-conscious judge. Judges favor different things in dogs, and

Many bull-breeds of today are getting a bad rap. The Dogo Argentino has been outlawed in the United Kingdom in order to stop importation.

Though not a well-known breed, the Alapaha Blue Blood Bulldog is a "natural" bulldog. This is Marcel owned by Lana Lou Lane, the originator of the breed.

the mistake is breeding to satisfy what can only be a purely subjective opinion. It must be said that, in general, if a dog has no work to do that requires breeding for physical ability, then showing and breeding for shows is too often counterproductive to canine health. People have bred many breeds into a truly sorry state, and only now are some breed clubs acting against inherent hip, eye, breathing and skin disorders. When looking at Bulldogs, ask yourself which, in your opinion, could bait a bull and which could not. It is beside the point to claim that the dog will never be called on to bait a bull; the point is that if a Bulldog is to go by that name, it must be able to do the job its title indicates. Just as a Pointer is able to point or a German Shepherd to herd sheep, a Bulldog must be able to do his work. If it cannot, quite simply it is not a Bulldog.

A bulldog bitch bred by Mr. Clifford Derwent— "the First" in Bulldog breeding.

The Lazarus Effect

After all the damage done to the Bulldog by breeders who need a dog to do no more than walk 2 yards in a show-ring and whose exercise regime for this once most supreme athlete is a five-minute walk followed by a long sleep, it might come as a surprise to discover that there are people who still regard the Bulldog as worthy of respect. These people, whose love of the breed cannot be questioned, usually begin their love affair with the modern Bulldog. At some point, however, the health, condition and limitations of the modern animal became too much to ignore. Rather than make excuses, they tore up the rule book and set out with sincere and decent intentions to do something positive for their breed. Not all those who tried were successful and not all those who claim success used what everyone would consider to be the right stock or approach.

There is no doubt that the following account of breeders excludes many good honest people. For that we have already apologized and do so again.

CLIFFORD DERWENT

To call anyone in dog breeding "The First" is some-what misleading, but when speaking of Clifford Derwent we can use the term quite genuinely. Clifford Derwent hit the headlines in the early 1970s by using his maiden speech at his first Kennel Club meeting as an elected member to attack the way breed standards all too often destroy breed health. But long before then he was into bull-breeds. An architect in pre-war

London, his first dog was a Bullmastiff. On return to
England after the war, he went back to Bullmastiffs
and began breeding them in partnership with Doris
Mullin. By the early 1950s he owned some 30
Bullmastiffs, including at least one champion. Then, in
1953 he gave up the breed. Disillusioned with the
prevalence of leukemia in the breed, he set out to do
something about it but found himself opposed by
others in Bullmastiff circles. It was then that he made
his first enemies, but not his last. The catalyst that
makes Clifford Derwent important in Bulldog history
came shortly after his abandonment of Bullmastiffs.
While walking his wife Joan's Bulldog on a beach in the
south of England, he was forced to carry the exhausted
dog home after it collapsed in a state of some paralysis.
The incident so upset Derwent that he found himself
looking at other specimens of the breed and found
them all wanting. Disgusted by the state of the canine
symbol of Britain, he set out with the idea of breeding
a version of the old, more active Bulldog. He searched
for a dog that looked as close to "Rosa," the 1820s
model for the original Philo Kuon standard, that he
could find. The plan being to cross this dog back to
pure-bred Bulldogs and correct the faults in the breed.
He found his ideal outcross dog in the company of two
plumbers one night in London. The dog was a Kennel-
Club-registered Staffordshire Bull Terrier, standing tall
and weighing 92 pounds. He bought him and began a
breeding program that was to produce what became
known as the "Regency Bulldog." By mating the
Stafford with pure Bulldogs and mating the best pups
back to more pure Bulldogs he diluted the outcross
enough to permit Kennel Club registration. He now

had big, strong, healthy Bulldogs, Kennel Club registered and breathing properly, but they did abysmally in the show ring. Many in the Bulldog fraternity ostracized Derwent, and other breed clubs, fearful of what might happen if such mavericks were allowed to succeed, followed suit. The Kennel Club refused to back Derwent's bid for separate registration of his dogs as "Regency Bulldogs" and after a while he gave up.

The Bulldogs he bred were never sold despite being highly sought after and have now disappeared. However, in Bulldog history, Derwent's efforts are generally recognized as the first attempts in modern times to redefine the Bulldog.

DAVID LEAVITT

In 1971, in the United States, David Leavitt began a breeding program aimed at creating a dog with the looks of the 18th century Bulldog of England. His aims

David Leavitt's breeding program attempts to recreate the Bulldog of the 18th century.

and methods differed from those of Clifford Derwent of England in that he used American breeds and had slightly different ideals in mind. Where Derwent sought the "re-creation" of a dog that once existed, Leavitt sought the making of an original breed. Using period statues and pictures, Leavitt set about "back-breeding" to capture much the same look, though in a bigger and more aggressive looking animal. He states however, that he in no way sought the old Bulldog temperament (or that questionably described by commentators of the time), instead seeking a placid and friendly dog that would none the less react if required to do so. He terms this character "courage and determination, without being overly aggressive," which might be said to be the typical Bulldog nature.

David Leavitt strives for the typical Bulldog nature in his breeding program—courage and determination, without being overly aggressive.

David Leavitt with an Olde English Bulldogge.

As his animals attest, David Leavitt has achieved the making of a handsome bulldog breed.

Using a line-breeding scheme developed by the State University of Ohio, Leavitt set about his program with complete professionalism. The scheme required a nucleus of three unrelated adult dogs, two male and one female. Female pups from the first cross are bred to the second male, thereafter females are bred back to uncles throughout the generation. He used two unrelated trios in his program in order that outcrosses would be possible. All the dogs he selected were from bull-breeds and his animals now breed to type. The foundation is 50% Bulldog and the other 50% is Bullmastiff, American Pitbull Terrier, and American Bulldog in equal measure. As his animals attest, he has achieved the making of a handsome Bulldog breed and his dogs are self-whelping, easy breathing, self-mating in that they need no artificial insemination, athletic to a greater degree, and have life spans of around 11 years.

Leavitt's dogs have proved themselves loving and reliable family pets and are trainable and honest. They get on well with children (and other animals) and are genetically free of defects. He has set his own standard but he insists that health be put above aesthetics every time. As Leavitt says: *It was always my intention to create a bulldog that served people, rather than a bulldog that needed serving by people.*

LOLLY WILKINSON

On Vancouver Island, British Columbia, Canada, Lolly Wilkinson has been breeding a strain of Bulldogs for many years that remains true to a much older type. These dogs originate from those taken to Canada when it was first settled by the British, and type has

David Leavitt's Olde English Bulldogges are much more athletic than the accepted modern Bulldog.

Lolly Wilkinson has been breeding bulldogs that remain true to a much older type.

been preserved by aspiring to function and historical correctness rather than fashion and kennel club standards.

Lolly Wilkinson's dogs are fit, healthy and athletic, and her rigorous efforts and steadfast refusal to compromise have resulted in a Bulldog not recognized by kennel clubs but sought after as a true representative of the breed. It is worth noting that Lolly Wilkinson does not show her dogs and that they are bigger and heavier, without being over-big or over-heavy, than the commonly accepted modern Bulldog. They weigh in at between 50 and 75 pounds and stand 17 to 19 inches at the shoulder. As such they would be penalized in kennel club showrings, and those in Bulldog circles whose only interest is in showing their specimens maintain that her dogs are not Bulldogs at all. However, as with all the "alternative" breeders, we must let the dogs speak for themselves. And as Ms. Wilkinson attests, in Canada, outside the showring, the Bulldog is alive and well.

JAN DIRK VAN GINNEKE

Jan Dirk van Ginneke, a representative of the Animal Research Foundation based in Holland, has been involved with animals for over 18 years. Indeed, he claims "dog" talk was one of the main attractions that

Wildbunch's Midget bred by Jan Dirk van Ginneke.

Jan Dirk van Ginneke with Harmony.

It is clear from his dogs that Jan Dirk van Ginneke is an alternative Bulldog breeder to be respected.

Wildbunch's Fury, a female bred by Jan Dirk van Ginneke.

Wildbunch's Melody, bred by Jan Dirk van Ginneke, loves to swim.

Two of Jan Dirk van Ginneke's alternative Bulldogs, Wildbunch's Fury and Wildbunch's Bundy.

drew he and his future wife together when they met in a disco nearly 20 years ago. They live just outside Rotterdam, in what they call their "own little paradise," and it is there that Jan and Betty carry out their breeding program. Jan's interest in the Bulldog began at an early age, but again the inherent health problems set him on a course that ended with a breeding program intended to produce a deliberately altered Bulldog.

He used a modern Bulldog and an American Staffordshire Bull Terrier as his foundation, then concentrated future breeding on mating back to modern Bulldogs. He later imported an American Bulldog from John D. Johnson in Georgia for the purpose of outcrossing. Jan Dirk van Ginneke has a knowledge of

Jan Dirk van Ginneke is adamant that any pups he does not keep will only be supplied to responsible owners.

Wildbunch's Rose bred by Jan Dirk van Ginneke.

One of Jan Dirk van Ginneke's puppies, Zwettler's Junior, at seven weeks of age.

the bull-breeds that is almost encyclopedic and used his own commitment and that of his wife, Betty, to good effect. What is clear from his dogs is that he is an alternative Bulldog breeder to be respected. He is adamant that any pups he does not keep will only be supplied to responsible people, and it will be interesting to observe his further achievements as the breeding program develops.

KEN MOLLETT

It is said that London is haunted by the ghostly hounds of Herne the Hunter and that in places to the east of the city, where the Isle of Dogs is bounded by the Thames, the noise of these hounds can still on certain nights be heard. The legend is ancient, as London is ancient, and though you may never hear these hounds, it is believable that some people may have.

Boatswain, bred by Ken Mollett, at three years of age.

Ken Mollett with a three-week-old Boatswain.

At night, when the hustle and bustle of the city dies down, if one stands on the banks of the Thames and breathes the scent of the river, you can almost hear the panting breath of the Bulldogs of yesterday. You can still drink in pubs that stood when Paris Garden flourished and walk narrow streets called Paris Garden and Bear Garden, both on the south bank of the Thames by Blackfriars and Southwark Bridges.

Old barges still litter the waterway and streets lined with warehouses centuries old clutter the darkness. Only a little imagination is needed to hear the voices and commotion of the men and women, children and dogs, carriages and horses as they jostle to the ghostly

A six-week-old pup bred by Ken Mollett.

One of Ken Mollett's Victorian Bulldogs, Basil, at eight months old.

Head and body study of an accepted modern Bulldog.

Head and body study of Ken Mollett's breeding.

theaters and markets, circuses and baits, fairs and jousts. Indeed there are still pubs where nighttime sees variety acts that could have graced Shakespeare's era, or Wren's, or Blake's or even Caesar's.

For all the technology and advances of modern society, London is unchanged. On the surface it is a thriving modern metropolis and one of the Earth's biggest cities, yet beneath its thin veneer it is still the same as it ever was. The lapping of the night river on the long steps still sighs of far away places

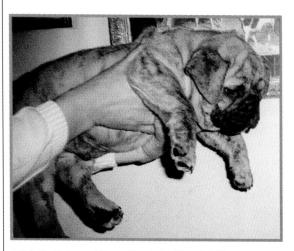

This is Prince Albert, bred by Ken Mollett, at ten weeks of age.

and different times. In the midst of all the clamor, there are still silences.

Somehow the Bulldog belongs in this ghostly place. The most important feature of the Bulldog is its spirit, and its spirit is older than our language. To see a Bulldog as just a dog is not to see it all. For these reasons there is something uniquely right and fitting in the existence of a breeder called Ken Mollett.

For over 15 years, on the edges of the city, a breeding program has been undertaken. Begun as the hobby of a Bulldog lover tired of the ills and ails that saw several of his earlier Kennel Club-registered Bulldogs living feeble lives and meeting untimely deaths, the program developed into a fully fledged campaign to turn back the clock on the Bulldog's health.

The most noticeable difference between the accepted modern Bulldog, shown here, and Ken Mollett's Bulldog is size. Ken Mollett's Bulldogs are bigger, weighing in at 70–75 pounds.

With the passing of the years, Graham Woods and Ken Mollett's brother Derek, both early partners in the program, gave up or sought other goals, but Ken persisted. Using only bull-breeds registered with the Kennel Club of Great Britain, and anchoring his program firmly on the modern Bulldog, he set about crossing Staffords, Bullmastiffs, Bull Terriers and the healthiest Bulldogs he could find. There were disappointments and mistakes, much hardship and little reward. He selected carefully and every animal used was the best available.

Working to old photographs, statues, written descriptions and engravings, he set out to remake the dog pictured in Victorian times. He called this dog the Victorian Bulldog; the type is fixed on and the dogs are breeding regularly to that type. As a rule, they all self-whelp; they have no inherited defects;

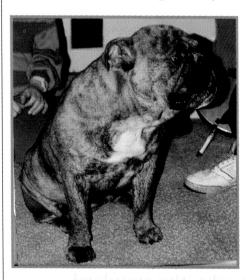

Tareth, a brindle bitch bred by Ken Mollett.

they can walk for miles, in fact they demand good exercise; and they are all reliable and placid pets. They are Bulldogs through and through, and any who doubt the fact are seeing with jaundiced eyes.

Any doubts that Ken Mollett has recreated the Victorian Bulldog, a stunning, fit, healthy and pleasant-natured dog that is the image of animals not seen for over 90 years, are dispelled when these dogs are met. Their temperament is unquestionably perfect. Raised with his own children, any dog with less than perfect temperament was most definitely discarded. They are placid, friendly and tolerant, yet watchful and loyal.

Nothing new has been added to Bulldogs by Mollett, just a few crucial things re-awakened. They're different to modern Bulldogs, most noticeably in size. They are bigger, weighing in at around 70—75 pounds, but just as a Giant Schnauzer is as much a Schnauzer as the Standard Schnauzer, the Victorian Bulldogs are as much Bulldogs as anything registered with the American Kennel Club or the Kennel Club of Great Britain. And of course, the health of the dog was always put above aesthetic considerations.

Ken Mollett has set a standard for his Victorian Bulldogs that is very close to the Philo Kuon standard that originated the breeding of Bulldogs to a type fixed by showing rather than work. Mollett insists, however, that since the health of his dogs is more

Ken Mollett's son Joe with The Baron.

important than their looks, the standard should be viewed as a blueprint, not a straight jacket.

That the dogs are bigger than their relatives registered at the kennel clubs is a by-product rather than an aim of the program. As Ken Mollett often points out, any fool can breed a big dog and if all that is wanted is a big "bully" type animal, it would have been achievable with a lot less

Ken Mollett's son Neal with The Baron.

effort. The hard thing is breeding a Bulldog that is of Victorian type yet with enough modern Bulldog retained to make it recognizable to contemporary eyes and with a temperament that is ideally suited to a family environment.

Whether the Bulldog clubs and, more essentially, the kennel clubs have the grace to acknowledge what Ken Mollett has done has yet to be seen. So far official recognition has been denied, but it is hoped that with the emergence of the Victorian Bulldogs on British streets, officialdom will come to see their value.

What is without doubt is that through the efforts and dedication of Ken Mollett, as all who meet the dogs will testify, a special Bulldog has come home.

Ken Mollett's Bulldogs possess a temperament that is ideally suited to a family environment. This is Joe Mollett with Boatswain.

As all Ken Mollett's Bulldogs will testify, a special Bulldog has come home.

Ken Mollett's Standard for the Victorian Bulldog
General Appearance

A medium size, smooth-coated dog with a solid but active countenance. Large headed and thick boned, only to the point that it does not impede vigor. Broad muzzled and short faced, but not so excessive as to interfere with breathing.

Hindquarters somewhat higher and not as heavy as foreparts, but not so as to destroy the symmetry of a muscular athlete.

Temperament

Although fierce and formidable in appearance, the dog must possess a steady, loyal and dependable nature, being bold without aggression, with a proud air of "nothing to prove."

Head

The head should be large but not exaggerated out of proportion to body.

Cheeks rounded and extended sideways beyond the eyes.

Face measured from front of cheek-bone to tip of nose, long enough for unhindered breathing. Muzzle broad and turning up. Undershot but not to excess.

Nostrils large and wide, black preferred but dudley acceptable.

Flews broad and hanging over lower jaw at sides.

Teeth canines large and wide apart, with ideally six smaller, even teeth between. A square bite (not wry).

Eyes from the front, set low and wide apart. Neither bulging or sunken and on no account should the haw be visible.

Ears no preference to rose or button. On no account erect or cropped.

Ezmarelda, foundation bitch in Ken Mollett's breeding program, is an excellent mother.

Neck

Thick, strong and arched, with loose skin forming dewlap on each side.

Body

Shoulders broad and deep. Rounded ribs with a wide chest narrowing towards the loins without exaggeration. The belly should be well tucked up and on no

Ken Mollett has recreated the Victorian Bulldog—a stunning, fit, healthy and pleasant-natured dog that is the image of animals not seen for over 90 years.

account rotund. A roach back is desired as long as it is not carried to excess or makes the dog look deformed. Forelegs muscular, straight and wide apart, not bandy or curved. Elbows away from ribs. Pasterns straight and strong. Hindlegs strong and muscular. Hocks slightly bent. Feet round and compact.

Tail

Either straight, turning down, or screwed. Not carried above back or docked.

Coat

Short.

Colour

In order of preference: Red brindle. All other brindles. Solid white or pied. Solid red. Fawn or fallow. On no account black, or black and tan.

Size

Males:	17 –19 inches	70–75 pounds.
Females:	16 –18 inches	55–65 pounds.

Vero Shaw's Bulldog

For serious students of the Bulldog history, I have decided to reprint in full Chapter Ten of the often quoted Book of the Dog by Vero Shaw. What one must remember is the power of the written word in the days before radio and television. I find this chapter fascinating for its derision of the Spanish Bulldog and its alien blood; but not a single mention of the Pug blood that we know was used. It has happened time and time again when people only report and fabricate history to suit their own often misguided theories. The paragraph on the cruel practice of faking shows how the unnatural pushed in face was so desirable for the show ring.

THE BULL-DOG

Allusion having been made to the great antiquity of the Bull-dog in the chapter on the Mastiff, it will be unnecessary for us to recapitulate in the present instance what we said before concerning the claims of rival breeds to be regarded as the most ancient variety of British dog. Few, however, can be found who refuse to award the Bull-dog the honor of being considered our *national dog*, for no variety of the canine species is so universally identified, both at home and abroad, with Great Britain, as the subject of the present article. Bull-dog pluck and endurance are qualifications eagerly cherished by Englishmen of all classes; and it would be manifestly unjust to deprive this dog of the title which has been so universally awarded him.

No breed of dog has provoked more discussion than the subject of this chapter, and in no canine controversy has party feeling run so high, and so many uncomplimentary epistles been exchanged. The result, however, of the angry battle of words has been so far a gain to the breed as to cause a perceptible increase in the number and quality of the exhibits at the principal shows, and, in the year 1875, it was the means of inducing several breeders to unite, and form the New Bull-dog Club, which has drawn up the scale of points now received by the vast majority of breeders throughout the country, whether members of the Club or not. Now that there seems to be some sort of unanimity between the various schools, the variety bids fair to prosper; and though from its excitable temperament the Bull-dog is not likely, in spite of its many high claims upon public favor, to be a general pet, it is gratifying to all lovers of this our national dog when they find it slowly, though surely, emerging from the hands of the residuum of the canine world, and taking its proper place in the kennels of a superior class of breeders and exhibitors. The gain to the dog will, we believe, be immense, for in the unhappy position into which it had fallen the Bull-dog had but slender opportunities of proving to the world that its intelligence was at least equal to that of the average run of dog. Chained up for weeks and months in damp cellars or dark confined hutches in miserable alleys, what chance had the poor brute of developing even that ordinary degree of sagacity which is expected to be found in an animal endued with sight and instinct? What possibility could there be that a creature so treated could beget offspring inheriting any of the better mental qualities which are naturally present in the Bull-dog, and which are developed in many dogs now before the public, whose lot has been cast in happier places than the habitation of a low scoundrel whose blow preceded his command, and who only noticed his wretched companion when desirous of participating with him in some revolting piece of cruelty in which the dog, through his indomitable courage, was destined to take a conspicuous part? How the Bull-dog ever came to be so nearly monopolized by this class of individual is capable of explanation by the theory that when bull-baiting ceased to be a fashionable recreation in this country, yet before it was absolutely prohibited by law, the sport was carried on by the lower classes, and the dog naturally came into their possession, there to remain until the efforts that were periodically made to extricate it should at last succeed.

The antiquity of this breed is indisputable, mention being made of it by Edmond de Langley, in his work, the "Mayster of Game," the MS. of which we have consulted in the British Museum. It is there alluded to by him under the title of Alaunt, and is subdivided by him into three classes; but perhaps it may be as well to give the description as contained in the "Mayster of Game:"—

"Alaunt is a manner and nature of houndes, and the good Alauntz ben the which men clepyn Alauntz gentil. Other then byn that amen clepyn Alauntz ventreres. Other byn Alauntz of the bocherie. Thei that ben gentile shuld be made and shape as a greyhounde, evyn of alle thinges, sauf of the heved, the whiche shuld be greet and short." After some further remarks, this same god is said to gladly "renne and bite the hors. Also thei renne at oxen and at sheep, at swyne, and to alle othere beestis, or to men, or to othere houndes, for men hav seyn Alauntz sle her maystir"; and, furthermore, they are described as being "more sturdy than eny other maner of houndes."

The second class of this dog is thus noticed:— "That other nature of Alauntz is clepid ventreres, almost thei bene shapon as a greyhounde of ful shap, thei hav grete hedes, and greet lippes, and greet eeris. And with

A northern England dog club in the early part of the 19th century.

such men helpeth hem at the baityng of a boole, and atte huntynge of a wilde boor. Thei holde fast of here nature..."

The third division:— "The Alauntz of the bocherie is soch as ye may alle day see in good tounes that byn called greet bochers houndis. Thei byn good for the baytyng of the bulle and huntyng of the wilde boor, whedir it be w'greihoundis at the tryste w'rennyng houndis at abbay with inne the coverte."

Whatever distinction there may have been between the above three varieties of Alaunt in the days of Edmund de Langley, and though the anonymous writer on the works of Arrian described these as above, and only attributes to the first two varieties an admixture of pure Celtic blood, it appears to us that the Alaunt is without a doubt the parent strain from which the present Bull-dog is descended; and although the Mastiff is alluded to by Edmund de Langley in his work, in addition to the three varieties of Alauntz, we can still discover no cause for altering our previously expressed opinion (see chapter on Mastiffs) that the Bull-dog and Mastiff originally sprang from the same origin—viz., the Mastive or Bandogge, which is alluded to in Dr. Caius's book and has been before quoted in this work on the article on Mastiffs. Before leaving the subject of the "Mayster of Game," we desire to impress upon our readers three times contained in the extracts we have quoted: first, the dog was *short*-faced; secondly he was used to bait the bull; and thirdly, when he attacked it or other animals he *hung on*. The first and third of these characteristics are present to a remarkable extent in the Bull-dog of the present day.

In the work of Dr. Caius, written in the reign of Queen Elizabeth, mention is made of the Mastive or Bandogge, as being a dog "stuborne, eagre, burthenous of body (and therefore but of little swiftness), terrible and fearefull to behold," and which "alone, and wythout anye help at al, he pulled down first an huge beare, then a parde, and last of al a lyon, each after other before the Frenche King in one day." This description of Caius's, relating as it does to the Mastive, which has already been alluded to in the

"Mayster of Game" as a peaceable dog, only tends to strengthen our previous conviction that the two breeds, Alaunt and Mastiff, had by some means or other become amalgamated, only to be again separated by the later breeders to suit the requirements of the times in the manner we have before suggested.

A postcard from the early 1900s.

In the later works on the dog, mention of the Bull-dog is frequently occurring, and all writers are unani-mous in their praises of the dog's courage and boldness in attack. The matter of size has provoked more discussion than any other feature in connection with this dog—one party holding out for a great, lumbering, long-faced dog, nearly as big as the bull itself, and destitute of any pretenses to symmetry in its appearance; the other side advocate the claims of a large-skulled dog, of medium size—forty to fifty pounds—with the short head described by Edmund de Langley in the "Mayster of Game." As regard the respective merits of the two dogs there can, in an unprejudiced mind, be no hesitation in accepting the latter as the correct type. In the first place, supposing bull-baiting were again in vogue, what could be the use of using a large dog for the work when a small one can do it as well if not better? Secondly, even assuming for the moment that a hundred years ago or more the Bull-dog was the coarse-looking creature some of its admirers say it was, is this breed to be the only one in which no refine-ment is ever to appear? We do not hold with improving a breed off the face of the earth, and have no sympathy with those who attempt to do so; but if we could by any surgical operation bring ourselves to look upon some specimens we see at shows as representing the correct type, we should gladly avail ourselves of any opportunity for refining and improving the breed.

Again, in baiting the bull the dogs usually approached him crawling along the ground on their bellies, and the result would be that a large dog would stand a much greater chance of falling a victim to his antagonist's horns. In this opinion we are supported by written authority as well as by all the gentlemen who have had personal experience of bull-baiting with whom we have conversed on the subject. Amongst these is Mr. Leare, of Sunbury-on-Thames, who, though born in the first year of the present century, still puts to shame many of his juniors when handling the rod or gun, and who, in his youth, was present at bull-baitings innumerable. According to this gentleman, a bull was rarely slaughtered in Devonshire—for this is Mr. Leare's

native county—in former times without being first
subjected to the ordeal of baiting by dogs in every
respect resembling the Bull-dog as hereafter described:—The weight was between forty pounds and
fifty pounds, a larger one being suspected—no doubt
correctly—of having a Mastiff cross; and a short *retroussé*

A postcard from the early 1900s. Note the wording at the bottom.

nose was eagerly sought after as enabling the dog to
breathe when hanging on to the nose of the bull.

   During the last century it was the almost invariable
custom to bait a bull before slaughtering him; and it
was not solely on account of the "sport" entailed that
this proceeding was in vogue, for there was a prevailing
opinion that the flesh of a bull which had been baited
was improved in quality by the exertions which he had
to put forth in defending himself from his canine
assailant. Whether this theory was correct or not we
decline to decide; but very much the same idea is in

existence in the present day as regards hares, many people being of the opinion that the flesh of a coursed hare is far superior to that of one which has been shot.

Some difference of opinion has risen, too, as regards the length of the face in this breed, a statement having appeared in print to the effect that the nose should not be too short, and rather implying that a medium length from the skull to the tip of the nose was desirable. Such heresy against the accepted opinions of all recognized authorities could only emanate from the pens of those either completely ignorant of the subject upon which they were writing, or else in possession of a strain which differed materially from the British Bull-dog, under whatever designation they might appear.

Attempts have also been made to improve the breed of Bull-dogs existent in the country by the addition of a so-called Spanish cross. What was the precise advantage to be derived from the introduction of the blood of a Spanish Bull-dog we are at a lost to conjecture, as the animal selected for resuscitating our national dog was the notorious Toro, a red-brindled dog, with cropped ears, weighing some 90 lbs., and displaying many indications of a Mastiff cross. From what we have heard from various sources it appears that Toro, in spite of the assertion in the Kennel Club Stud Book to the effect that both his parents were pure-bred Spanish Bull-dogs, is supposed by many of his admirers to be descended from some English Bull-dogs which were exported from this country to Spain several years ago. Now, assuming for the sake of argument that both these theories can be correct, we still fail to discover from the appearance of Toro how he could possibly be of service in improving the Bulldog as it now exists in this country, the main object of successful exhibitors being to eliminate all traces of the Mastiff in their dogs, as such would tend to place great obstacles in their success under a competent judge. That Toro may possibly be a perfect specimen of the Spanish Bull-dog we will not attempt to deny, for we consider the breed apocryphal, but we unhesitatingly assert that the introduction of his blood into our English kennels must inevitably be attended by the most pernicious consequences, and it is to be hoped that breeders will adhere to the blood that our ancestors possessed, without being led astray by the wiles of the charmers, charm they never so wisely.

In the year 1874 Mr. Theodore Bassett, the well-known Fox-terrier judge, astonished the Bull-dog world by importing an "African" Bull-dog, and exhibiting him at our shows. This dog, Leon by name, had, like Toro, been deprived of his ears, and though superior to the latter in every Bull-dog characteristic, was very soon after his first appearance relegated, by the good sense of his master, to the foreign dog class, where his fine proportions have been fully recognised, as his many successes testify.

Having thus warned our readers against attempting to improve the Bull-dog by a foreign cross, it behooves us to likewise put them on their guard against the great, coarse, lumbering-looking dogs sometimes met with at shows. These animals, though possibly in themselves showing little trace of Mastiff blood to the uninitiated, cannot deceive a practical breeder, and the result of an alliance between one of them and a young inexperienced admirer's brood bitch will almost invariably be years of disappointment on the show bench, coupled with vain endeavors at home to rid the strain of the noxious taint brought in by the injudicious selection of the founder of the stud.

The Bull-dog has undoubtedly suffered considerably from his association with the lower classes of the community; and amongst other undesirable practices which have crept in connection with the breed is the abominable mutilation resorted to by some breeders in order to shorten the length of the upper jaw, and turn the nose well up. In their endeavours to attain the above object the operators in the first instances sever the middle and two side lip-strings which connect the upper lip of the dog with the gum; when this is satisfactorily accomplished, a sort of small wooden block, hollowed so as to fit the face, is applied to the outside of the upper jaw in front, and being smartly hit with a mallet, has the effect of compressing the bone and cartilage of the nose as desired. Naturally the operation has to be performed when the unfortunate puppies are of an early age, and the bones and muscles of their faces are soft and susceptible of compression. An instrument technically termed the "Jacks" is then applied, and has the effect of causing the mutilated parts to remain in their new and abnormal position. No words can express our repugnance at the horrible cruelty thus inflicted upon the unhappy puppies by the wretches who wantonly inflict such torture upon them, and no judge should award either prizes or commendations to a Bull-dog until he has perfectly satisfied himself that the dog has been spared the mutilation of "faking," as the operation is designated by the initiated. Unfortunately the detection of offenders is sometimes a matter of difficulty, and those credited with originating the practice have passed to the silent land beyond the reach of human laws; but considerable aid might be lent to honest exhibitors in their endeavours to stamp out this abominable scandal, if show committees were to appoint a really qualified veterinary inspector who understood the anatomy of a dog, and whose decision was to be final. As a case in point: when the Bull-dogs Bumble and Alexander were disqualified by the veterinary inspector at the Crystal Palace Show of 1876, the Committee of the Kennel Club actually permitted a further inspection to be made by another surgeon, who held no position in connection with the show, the result being that both dogs were pronounced "honest," and had their prizes restored them. Whether Bumble and Alexander were mutilated or not need not be the subject of discussion here; but we maintain that direct encouragement was unwittingly given to dishonest breeders by the Committee not supporting their own veterinary surgeon in the opinion he pronounced.

Amongst the best known owners, breeders, and exhibitors of the correct type of Bull-dog since the Birmingham Show of 1860 may be mentioned the names of Mr. J. Hinks, of Birmingham; the Lamphiers, father and son; Messrs. H. Brown, Stockdale; J. Percival, W. Macdonald, Jesse Oswell, H. Layton, P. Rust, Billy Shaw, J. Henshall, W. Page, R. Fulton, W.H. Tyser, R. Ll. Price, S.E. Shirley, M.P., G.A. Dawes of West Bromwich (in many but not all instances), J.W. Berrie, T.H. Joyce, W.G. Mayhew, Egerton Cutler, Vero Shaw, G. Raper, W. St. John Smyth, H.F. Procter, T. Meager, J. Turnham, C.E. Bartless, E.T. Hughes, R. Nicholas, W.W. Roger, Capt. Holdsworth, T. Verrinder, Sir William Verner, Bart., T. Alexander, R. Turton, the Duke of Hamilton (in some cases), and many others. All the above have either shown or bred first-class specimens of the breed, amongst which may be mentioned—King Dick, Dan, Michael (who was eaten during the siege of Paris), Romany, Punch, Beeswing, Bowler, Young Duke, Meg. Gipsy Queen, Maggie Lauder, Dido, Master Gully, Acrobat, Page's Bill, King, Neil, Smasher, Prince, Alexander, Baby, Billy, Gambler, Noble, Nettle, Sancho Panza, Slenderman, Sir. Anthony, Brutus, Rose, Donald, Alexander, and the famous Sheffield Crib.

Mr. George Raper, of Stockton-on-Tees, has kindly supplied us with the following notes on this breed:—

"The properties of the Bull-dog have been divided into some eighty or ninety points. To the late Jacob Lamphier, in conclave with friends who, like himself, made the Bull-dog an especial study, we are indebted for a most carefully compiled list of properties and points, which are as follows:—

"1. *The Ears.*–(1) Size: should be small. (2) Thinness. (3) Situation: they should be on the top of the head. (4) Carriage: they should be either "rose," "button," or "tulip" ears. The "rose" ear folds at the back; the tip laps over outwards, exposing part of the inside. The "button" ear only differs from the "rose" in the falling of the tip, which laps over in front, hiding the interior completely. The "tulip" ear is nearly erect; it is the least desirable form.

"2. *The Skull (exclusive of property No. 4).*—(1) Size: should be large. (2) Height: this should be great. (3) Prominence of the cheeks: they should extend well beyond the eyes. (4) Shortness (i.e., breadth in comparison to length). (5) Shape of forehead: it should be well wrinkled, and not prominent, as in the "King Charles" Spaniel.

"3. *The Eyes.*— (1) Colour; should be as nearly black as possible. (2) Shape of the opening of the lids: should be quite round. (3) Size; should be moderate. (4) Position: they should be quite in front of the head, as far from the ear and as near to the nose as possible— very far apart, but not so far as to interfere with point 3 of the second property, and neither prominent nor deeply set in the head. (5) Direction of the corners: they should be at right angles to a line drawn down the centre of the face.

"4. *The Stop. (this is an indentation between the eyes).*— (1) Depth. (2) Breadth. (3) Length: it should extend some considerable distance up the head.

"5. *The Face.*—(1) Shortness, measured from the front of the cheek bone to the end of the nose: this point cannot be carried to too great an excess. (2) Wrinkles: these should be deep, and close together. (3) Shape: the muzzle should turn upwards.

"6. *The Chop.*—(1) Breadth. (2) Depth. (3) The covering of the teeth: these should be perfect.

"7. *The Nose.*—(1) Size: should be large. (2) Should be black. (3) Width of nostrils.

"8. *The Termination of the Jaws.*—(1) Breadth: should be as great as possible. (2) Relative position: the lower jaw should project considerably in advance of the upper, so that the nose is very much set back, but not to such an extent as to interfere with point 2 of the sixth property. (3) Shape of the lower jaw: this should turn upwards.

"9. *The Neck.*—(1) Length: this should be moderate. (2) Thickness: should be considerable. (3) Shape: it should be well arched at the back. (4) Wrinkles and dewlap.

"10. *The Chest.*—(1) Width: this should be very great. (2) Shape: it should be deep and round.

"11. *The Body (exclusive of Property No. 10).*—(1) Shortness of back. (2) Width across back: this should be very great at the shoulders, and the spine should rise at the loins, falling again very much towards the stern, and forming an elegant arch. The ribs should be well rounded.

"12. *The Stern.*—(1) Fineness. (2) Length: this should be moderate. (3) Shape: a slight crook is no objection, but a screwed or knotted stern is a deformity. (4) Carriage: this should be downwards; the dog should not be able to raise it about the level of his back. (5) Situation this should be low down at the insertion.

"13. *The Fore-legs.*—(1) Stoutness: they should be very thick in the calves. (2) Shape; rather bowed. (3) Length: they should be short, more so than the hind legs, but not so short as to make the back appear long. (4) Width apart.

"14. *The Hind-legs (including stifles).*—(1) Length: should be moderate, but greater than that of the fore-legs, so as to elevate the loins. (2) Position: the hocks should approach each other, which involves the turning out of the stifles. (3) Roundness of the stifle.

"15. *The Fore-feet (including pasterns).*—(1) Shape: they should be moderately round, but well split up between the toes. (2) Prominence of the knuckles. (3) Position: they should be straight—that is, neither turned outward nor inwards. (4) Straightness of the pastern. (5) Size: they should be rather small.

"16. *The Hind-feet.*—(1) Shape: they are not expected to be so round as the fore-feet, but they should not be long like a terrier's; they should be well split up between the toes. (2) Prominence of the knuckles. (3) Position: they should be turned outwards. (4) Straightness of the pasterns. (5) Size: they should be rather small.

"17. *The Coat.*—(1) Fineness. (2) Shortness. (3) Closeness.

"18. *The Colour.*—(1) Uniformity: the colour should be "whole" (that is, unmixed with white), unless the dog be all white, which is, in that case, considered a "whole" colour. (2) Tint: this should be either red, red-smut (that is, red with black muzzle), fawn or fawn-smut, fallow or fallow-smut, brindled, white, or pied with any of those colours. (3) Brilliancy and purity.

"19. *General Appearance, Proportion, Carriage, and Size.*—(1) Proportion: no property should be so much in excess as to destroy the general symmetry of the dog. (2) The general appearance of the dog (that is, the impression that he makes as a whole on the eye of the judge). (3) Carriage: the dog should roll in his gait. He generally runs rather sideways. His hind-legs should not be lifted high as he runs, so that his hind-feet seem to skim the ground (4) Size: from about 20 lbs. to 60 lbs.

"Authorities differ regarding the original of the Bull-dog, but we may safely aver that the demand produced the supply, and as the favourite sport of James I. of England had its rise, reached its zenith, and declined, so the animals best suited for the purpose of bull-baiting were fostered in these islands, which now claim them as indigenous; but, the time arriving when the village cry of "No bull, no parson!" became fainter and fainter, as our civilisation increased, so the Bull-dog of our ancestors has degenerated or improved (as the taste of our readers may suggest) into an animal to be pampered and petted and carefully bred for points, to be admired by his owner, or to compete for honours on the show-bench of our many exhibitions. As the field trials for our sporting dogs have done much to encourage the improvement of their mental qualities, which were beginning to be neglected in the pursuit of symmetry of form for show purposes, so without the field day for the Bull-dog the qualities for which he was famous are fast disappearing, under the blighting influence of this enlightened age. His service to the butchers in catching and throwing down cattle—which he formerly did with surprisingly apparent ease, by seizing an ox by the nose, and either holding him perfectly still or throwing him on to his side at his master's command—is now out of date, with his more distant performances of baiting the bull, the lion in the Tower of London, and, in 1825, the lion at Warwick.

"The purpose for which the dog was formerly bred having disappeared, the admirers of the breed, being at a loss for a common object, have cultivated a variety of specimens, according to the taste—or perhaps, more correctly speaking, according to the accident—by which they attached themselves to this noble dog, whose character combines all the qualities his more distinguished owner can boast, and many which his less fortunate hater or admirer might well aspire to imitate.

"It is not my province here to narrate the many acts of intelligence and faithfulness performed by this oft-maligned section of the friend of man, although they would compare most favourably with those of any of the more esteemed.

"It is generally acknowledged that of all breeds none are more liable to deterioration than the Bull-dog. In a litter you seldom find more than one specimen up to the mark when arrived at maturity. This breed of dogs varies very much in appearance, and even now, but more especially a few years ago, the types in different parts of the country were very marked.

"The Birmingham district has long been noted for its Bull-dogs. The marked defects of its specimens are that they want greater depth from the nose to the bottom jaw, many being so thin as to approach what is termed in the fancy "monkey-faced." Many are also wanting in length and width of under-jaw, and with few exceptions they are greatly in want of larger noses.

"Nottingham is another district where this breed has been fostered, and here again you find a marked difference of type. Generally they have good limbs and body, good skull and large eyes, but many are spoiled by a "tulip" ear, and are, moreover, inclined to be "frog-faced"—a great defect. The types of the London dogs vary considerably.

In breeding it will therefore be seen that much depends upon the selection of a suitable sire for the bitch intended to be bred from. Most of our best specimens are undoubtedly inbred. No doubt Percival's Toss holds prior claims, he being the grandsire of the celebrated dog King Dick, whose pedigree shows close in-breeding; nevertheless, it is an undisputed fact that he can claim near relationship to the greater majority of the prize-takers of the present day.

"Were I breeding for size I should select a large roomy bitch and put her to a high quality dog, for I have almost invariably found the dog stamp the quality of the puppies. Experience has taught me that you cannot obtain the points you breed for from the first cross, but must breed in once, at least, to secure the improvement you seek. I am certainly an advocate for judicious in-breeding, believing it to be the much wiser plan to breed from reliable and good blood than to admit questionable blood into your strain."

Having endeavoured to enumerate the leading exhibitors, past and present, and some of their best-known dogs, we will pass on to the formation of the Bull-dog.

The *skull* of the Bull-dog is essentially one of the chief characteristics of the breed. It should be of as great a circumference as possible (19 inches in a dog and 17 $^1/_2$ inches in a bitch is a fair estimate for a dog of 50 lbs. and a bitch of 45 lbs. weight), square in shape, broad in front, not wedge-shaped, and carrying a quantity of loose skin, which should lie in a number of heavy wrinkles over the head and face.

The *jaws* are peculiar in formation, as the lower jaw projects a considerable distance beyond the upper, and has, in addition, an upward turn in front.

The *tusks*, or canine teeth, should be wide apart, and it is desirable that the front teeth should be regular, though this feature is absent in many of our best dogs.

The *upper jaw* is, as above stated, considerably shorter than the lower, and both should display unmis-takable signs of strength.

The *lips*, termed "chop" by the initiated, should be very loose and heavy, and of considerable circumfer-ence.

The *nose*, which must lay well back, in fact be as *retroussé* as it is possible to imagine, must be broad, large, moist, and perfectly black—a parti or flesh coloured nose (technically-called "Dudley") being in

the opinion of many good judges an absolute disqualification in competition.

The *eyes* should be large but not too full or goggle,
soft, round, and dark in colour, set as far apart as
possible, and at right angles to an imaginary line drawn
the centre of the skull-an oblique or "Chinaman's" eye
is a decided blemish.

The *stop*, or indentation between the eyes should be
both wide and deep, extending up the skull in a deep
furrow for a considerable distance (when this formation is
present the skull is said to be "broken up"), and if this
feature is absent it gives the dog's head an appearance of
roundness which is highly undesirable, and he is termed
"apple-headed" in consequence.

The *ears* should be small, and "rose" shaped—*i.e.,*
laying back so that the inside burr is visible. They are
set on wide apart at the *corners* of the skull; if set on
too much at the top the skull is narrow, and if too low
down the sides the head is rounded, and therefore it is
most desirable that the ears should be set on well at
the corners of the skull. The thinner they are, too, the
better. According to the Bull-dog Club a tulip (prick)
and button ear are admissible, but no judge could, if in
his senses, pass a dog with a tulip ear; and, for our own
part, a button ear would go greatly against a dog.

The *cheek bumps* at the base of the jaws should be
clearly defined in a three-year-old dog; but as this
feature is only to be satisfactorily obtained by age and
maturity, though it should always be present to a
certain extent, too much importance should not be
attached to this point in a very young dog.

The *neck* must be muscular, slightly curved, and
provided with a heavy double dewlap.

The *shoulders* sloping and strong, firmly set on, and very muscular.

The *chest* must be as *wide* and *deep* as possible, so as to give (in conjunction with the rounded fore-ribs) plenty of space for the heart and lungs to act in.

The *fore legs*, which are much shorter than the hind, should be very powerful and straight, though the large amount of muscle on the outside is liable to convey the impression that the dog is bow-legged, which he should not be. They should be turned out at the shoulders, so that the body can swing between them when in motion.

The *fore feet* should be straight at the pasterns, large, moderately round, with the toes well split up, arched, and rather splayed out.

The *body* should be very deep at the chest and must be of considerable girth, with round ribs, and has the appearance of being on an incline, which arises from the fore-legs being shorter than the hinder, and also from the peculiar formation of the back, which, in addition to being extremely short, rises from the shoulders to the loins and then slopes down to the stern, thus producing the *"roach"* or *"wheel"* back which is essentially present in a good Bull-dog.

The *loins* are powerful, well arched, and tucked up: a "cobby" body is undesirable in this breed.

The *stern* or tail, which must be set on low, must be short and very fine. A break or knot near the base is approved of, as it renders getting his tail up impossible, and a ring, or crooked tail, is sought after by many breeders.

The *hind legs*, as before stated, should be higher than the front ones, and they should turn well *out* at the stifles and feet, which causes the hocks to turn inwards, which is imperative, for a Bull-dog should be "cow-hocked" and not go wide behind. The feet are in shape longer than the front ones, and more compact.

Almost any *colour* is admissible in a Bull-dog except black, or black-and-tan. Blue is undesirable; and perhaps the following classification of colours represents their respective values in the eyes of the breeders:— Brindle-and-white, brindle, white, fallow or fawn smut (fallow or fawn with black muzzled), fallow or fawn pied, red, and, lastly, the blue-ticked dog; but where so much latitude is allowed, the colour of a Bull-dog must be left out in judging specimens, except in cases of equal merit, when a judge must naturally be guided by any special weakness he may entertain towards one particular colour.

The *coat* is short, and close, and if brushed the wrong way extremely harsh, though on being smoothed down it is soft and silky to the touch.

The *walk* or *action* of the Bull-dog is almost indescribable in its ungainliness. We ourselves, though glorying in our admiration of the breed, cannot but admit that its paces are the incarnation of all that is clumsy. His short and immensely powerful body swings between the Bull-dog's out-turned shoulders, his high hind legs appear to be pushing his chest out between his fore legs, whilst the peculiar formation of his stifles and hocks scarcely permit him to raise his hind feet off the ground, and the result is an action which partakes of the elements of a rush, a shuffle, and an amble, without fairly representing either.

In *temper* the Bulldog will bear comparison with any breed of dog. To his master especially, and those he knows, he is amiable, loving, and obedient, but he will not usually make friends with strangers all at once, and invariably, if ill-treated, proceeds to resent the injuries inflicted on him in hot haste. If properly brought up, and not teased or irritated, a pure Bull-dog is both a noble-looking and enjoyable companion, but when once roused to action by cruelty his indomitable pluck and reckless disregard of physical suffering renders him a most formidable antagonist to man or beast.

The *general appearance* of a Bull-dog is that of a comparatively small dog very heavy for his size, of immense power, and great squareness of head, whether looked at from in front or profile, with the body gradually tapering off toward the stern; in fact, a first glance at a Bull-dog stamps him as the possessor of a combination of strength and activity unmet with in any other dog.

Weight, about fifty pounds for a dog and forty-five pounds for a bitch. Of course, there are many first-rate specimens of considerably less weight than the above, and a few heavier; but most of the best dogs scale between forty-two and forty-eight pounds when in show form, and not too fat.

In regard to the dogs chosen for illustration in this work, Smasher is by Master Gully out of Nettle by Sir Anthony by Sheffield Crib; Master Gully by Briton out of Kitt, Briton by Saxon out of Duchess. He has won first Bristol, 1876; first Edinburgh, first Blaydon-on-Tyne, first Darlington, first Alexandra Palace, 1877. In 1878 he was not shown. In 1879 he has won first and medal Dublin, first Wolverhampton, first Hanover. His measurements have not been received by us complete, but a few of them are as follows: Girth of muzzle, 14 $^1/_2$ inches; girth of skull, 21 $^1/_2$ inches; girth of neck, 20 inches; weight, 43 lbs.

Doon Brae, the second subject of illustration, is without doubt the best dog under 40 lbs. now alive, and we question if, at his weight, his equal has ever been seen. He was bred by his owner, Captain Holdsworth, in 1876; and is by Sir Anthony out of Polly, by Vero Shaw's Sixpence out of Whiskey by Fulton's Falstaff out of Nosegay; Sir Anthony by Sheffield Crib out of Meg, by Old King Dick out of Old Nell, by Old Dan. Crib's pedigree is disputed, and therefore we do not give it. He has won first Bristol, first Crystal Palace, and first Alexandra Palace, 1878; and first Alexandra Palace, 1879. The measurements of Doon Brae are:—Tip of nose to stop, 1 inch; stop to occiput, 5 inches; length of back, 15 $^1/_2$ inches; girth of muzzle, 12 inches; girth of skull, 19 $^3/_4$ inches; girth of neck, 17 $^1/_2$ inches; girth of brisket, 32 $^1/_2$ inches; girth of chest, 28 inches; girth of loins, 20 $^1/_2$ inches; girth of hind-leg at stifle-joint, 11/$^1/_2$ inches; girth of fore-arm, 7 $^1/_4$ inches; girth of knee, 5 inches; girth of pastern, 4 $^1/_4$ inches; height at shoulders, 17 $^1/_2$ inches; height at elbows, 8 $^1/_2$ inches; height at top of loins, 18 inches; height, hock to ground, 5 inches; length of stern, 7 $^1/_4$ inches.

Mr. T. Meager's Bismarck, of whom we give a wood-cut, is a very typical specimen of the breed. He won first in the small-weight class at the Bull-dog Club's show in 1876, at the Alexandra Palace, and, like Doon Brae, is under 40 lbs.

Subjoined is the scale of points as drawn up by the New Bull-dog Club in 1875. They are based on the well-known Philo-kuon scale, and received the support of the leading breeders and exhibitors at the time when they were first published:—

Points	Details for consideration of Judge	Distribution of 100 marks for total individual points
General Appearance	Symmetrical formation; shape, make, style, action and fraish	10
Skull	Size, height, breadth, squareness of skull; shape, flatness, and wrinkles of forehead	15
Stop	Depth, breadth, and extent	5
Eyes	Position, shape, size, and colour	5
Ears	Position, size, shape, carriage, thinness	5
Face	Shortness, breadth, and wrinkles of face; breadth, bluntness, squareness and upward turn muzzle; position, breadth size, and backward inclination of top of nose; size, width, blackness of and cleft between nostrils	5
Chop	Size and complete covering of front teeth	5
Mouth	Width and squareness of jaws, projection and upward turn of lower jaw; size and condition of teeth, and if the six lower teeth are in an even row	5
Chest & neck	Length, thickness, arching, and dewlap of neck; width, depth and roundness of chest..........................	5
Shoulders	Size, breadth, and muscle	5
Body	Capacity, depth, and thickness of brisket; roundness of ribs	5
Back roach	Shortness, width at shoulders; and height, strength and arch at loins	5
Tail	Fineness, shortness, shape, position and carriage	5
Fore legs and feet	Stoutness, shortness, and straightness of legs, development of calves and outward turn of elbows; straightness and strength of ankles, roundness, size, and position of feet, compactness of toes, height and prominence of knuckles	5
Hind legs and feet	Stoutness, length, and size of legs, development of muscles, strength, shape, and position of hocks and stifles, formation of feet and toes as in forelegs and feet	5
Size	Approaching 50 lb.	5
Coat	Fineness, shortness, and closeness of coat; uniformity, purity, and brilliancy of colour..........................	5
	Total for perfection in all points	100
	JUDGE'S NET TOTALS	

Whilst thoroughly agreeing with the above scale as one by which Bull-dogs can be most satisfactorily judged, we propose adding another embodying our own ideas, being of the opinion that a standard of 50 points is more easy of application to this and every breed.

SCALE FOR JUDGING BULL-DOGS

	Value
Skull, size, and shape	10
Head and face	10
Neck, chest, and shoulders	10
Body	5
Legs, feet, and tail	10
General appearance	5
Total	50

A Bull-breed Guide

AMERICAN BULLDOG

The American Bulldog is recognized throughout the
USA as a rare breed and belongs in this book not
because it is new or a revision of the existing "modern"
Bulldog but because it is very old. The breed has been
preserved for many years in the southern states of
America, only recently emerging to become more
popular in the north.

These dogs are still used as working dogs in the deep
south, where they are employed against the wild boar
that roam the forests. For this duty the Bulldog needs
to weigh between 70 and 100 pounds, and while the
sport is unsavory to many eyes, it does serve a purpose.
The boar weigh in at around 400 pounds and are
armed with razor sharp tusks. Consequently, they are
both a nuisance and a danger to human beings.

Hounds are used to hunt and corner the boar, and
theoretically the Bulldogs are then brought into the
action to do single combat with the boar. They rush in
past the hounds, which are too afraid to attack the
boar, and take a hold on the face of the wild animal.
From then on the fight is not unlike an old English
bait.

One might not be in favor of such activities, but
blood sports of a different kind, though equally as
bloody, are part of life throughout most of the world.
That these dogs are capable of such savagery when
called on and make such excellent house pets at other
times leads one to believe that the descriptions of
savagery toward people of the old English Bulldog is

The American Bulldog is recognized throughout the United States as a rare breed.

exaggeration on the part of commentators. This exaggeration was probably due to a fear or awe of the baiting Bulldog.

The way the American Bulldog works also tends to belie the theory that the English Bulldog was ever bred down much below 70 pounds for the sake of baiting. The theory apparently being that too heavy a dog would tear off the flesh from the bull, and the dog, loose from the bull's face, would be exposed to a goring revenge. If the boar of 400 pounds is baited by a dog averaging 70 or 80 pounds, then a dog of equal weight would surely not be too big to bait a bull. Taken with the evidence that the bull and terrier crosses, created to be lighter and faster than the Bulldog, weighed in at around 40 pounds and that the Bullmastiff, which is 40% Bulldog, still weighs in excess of 100 pounds suggests that throughout history a working strain of Bulldog existed in England that was heavier and leggier than that used in the later shows.

If the American Bulldog serves no other purpose, it can be considered a living museum piece and studied as such. I believe, however, that the dog belongs in the modern world, as a family pet and companion, as surely as do the Bullmastiff, Dogue de Bordeaux, Old English Sheepdog, Cocker Spaniel or any number of other dogs.

One of the primary strains of American Bulldog is bred by John D. Johnson, a famous and much respected breeder who explains: *The American Bulldog is the same type of dog that began life in England in the 12th and 13th centuries, and led a baiting life until the 18th century when (with the outlawing of baiting) breeders in England started crossing them with other breeds. In 1733 the English purchased a large tract of land from the Creek Indians which is today known as Savannah, Georgia. English people started settling there and brought their Bulldogs with them. These dogs are known today as the American Bulldog.*

There are now a few kennels in other parts of the United States specializing in the breed and developing the dogs in obedience and working trials where they excel.

MASTIFF
A massive and proud dog, at first glance it may not be obvious why the Mastiff belongs in a book on the Bulldog. However, early Roman writing indicates that the two breeds were once considered to be of the same family. The Mastiff should have a tight frame, not

The Mastiff is a good-natured, noble and trustworthy breed. Photo by Isabelle Francais.

gangly or loose-limbed, and should move with the confidence of a powerful athlete. It stands between 27 and 30 inches at the shoulder and weighs around 185 pounds.

This is an ancient breed that lived before the Christian era and was famed for its strength and ferocity. It has never been a cart pulling dog, as other giant European breeds often were, nor a herding dog, although it might be said that the Mastiff would excel at both. Rather it was a war dog.

In 1415 at the Battle of Agincourt, a Mastiff bitch gained fame and mythical status by standing guard over her aristocrat master's body throughout the conflict. This is a demonstration of unmatched courage when one considers that the French armies were bearing down on the English with some 30,000

Mastiffs are huge dogs, weighing in at around 185 pounds. Photo by Isabelle Francais.

The Bullmastiff is a cross between the 18th century Bulldog and the Mastiff. Photo by Isabelle Francais.

mounted knights. The bitch was used as a foundation for kennels and her offspring exist even today.

Today's Mastiff is not a dangerous or even aggressive dog, when properly exercised and handled. It is a good natured, noble and trustworthy breed, though more suited to country than town. Naturally, should the Mastiff ever be called upon to meet a threat, it will do so unswervingly.

BULLMASTIFF

This dog is exactly what its name implies, a cross between the Bulldog of the 18th century and the Mastiff. It was deliberately bred for gamekeeping purposes, to protect the gamekeeper and run down and hold poachers.

Originally they were dark brindle or red in color, allowing them to move unseen in the dark. They are a strong dog, agile and more athletic than Bulldogs, fiercer and more aggressive than Mastiffs, or so was the plan of the 18th century.

Today's Bullmastiff is not a fierce dog and is well suited to a family home provided there is a strong master or mistress on hand to keep control. A good modern Bullmastiff stands between 24 and 27 inches at the shoulder and weighs around 100 pounds. Today's dog is less brawny and cobby than the animal made in the 1860s which was 40% Bulldog and 60% Mastiff.

Buy with great care and do not just go for the animals that have won championships at shows. These dogs still like to work, but short-sighted breeding and judging has taken many animals away from what the Bullmastiff was supposed to be. Seek out athletes with good family health records, not just show winners, and buy only from stock that has an impeccable temperament. Your Bullmastiff should be able to move with ease amid country estates, keeping on the move all night or day in all weathers and running down poachers. If a Bullmastiff can't do that, it's not a Bullmastiff.

BULL TERRIER

Along with the Bulldog, the Bull Terrier is probably one of the most instantly recognizable dogs in the world. Strong, tightly muscled and with that incredible egg shaped head, he is a fighting dog.

Bred by the Bulldog fancier James Hinks of Birmingham, England, in the 1850s, the Bull Terrier has lost nothing over the last century. Thanks to the patronage of Raymond Oppenheimer and others of his ilk, the

With his egg-shaped head, the Bull Terrier is probably one of the world's most instantly recognizable dogs in the world. Photo by Isabelle Francais.

breed was further developed before, during and after World War II.

James Hinks was no slouch when it came to dogs, and apart from breeding wonderful Bulldogs and preferring the old baiting dogs to the increasingly popular show dog, he decided he could improve the Bull and Terrier fighting dog too. To do this he used baiting-bred Bulldogs and the now extinct English White Terrier. His dogs won at the shows and when challenged, won in the fighting pit.

As an all-around dog, the Bull Terrier is many people's favorite animal. But be warned, the terrier in the Bull Terrier is strong and still very present. This is a comical, fun-loving, adoring dog but also singled minded, stubborn, sharp and determined. Some say

The Bull Terrier was developed by crossing baiting-bred Bulldogs and the now extinct English White Terrier. Photo by Robert Smith.

The small, strong, tightly muscled Staffordshire Bull Terrier is the dog that ruled the rat pits in the England of yesteryear. Photo by Robert Smith.

"eccentric." The Bull Terrier, especially the male, is not a beginner's dog. While its temperament makes it ideal as a companion for children, the speed it moves its head and the boisterousness of its play can lead to accidents. Never excite your Bull Terrier and never try to make him tough. If you do, you'll reap the whirlwind.

STAFFORDSHIRE BULL TERRIER

The Staffordshire Bull Terrier is a fine, strong, small and tightly muscled dog that fits in well with a family environment. Standing between 14 and 16 inches at the shoulder and weighing (for show purposes) up to 38 pounds, this is the dog that ruled the rat pits in the England of yesteryear.

Perhaps, more than any other breed, the Staffordshire Bull Terrier comes in many sizes and shapes. Photo by Isabelle Francais.

The "Staffy" is athletic and willing, devoted and proud. The sizes given in the breed standard are guidelines only, and perhaps more than any other breed the Staffordshire Bull Terrier comes in many sizes and shapes. The fighting instinct is great in this dog and its willingness, indeed almost desperation, to have a fight means it must always be well controlled. Like its bigger cousin, the Bull Terrier, the "Staffy" is an excellent pet, if you don't mind its eccentricities. Some people have said this dog, like the Bull Terrier, is a shark on legs, and to see how some walk on the lead one understands why. However, there are so many variations in the Stafford breed that if some are sharks on legs, others are pike on stubs. The Staffordshire Terrier is a great dog for all the family, a tireless companion, a trustworthy addition to the home and a fearless guardian.

IRISH STAFFORDSHIRE BULL TERRIER

This is a little known dog outside of Ireland and parts of England. It was bred for use in the dog fighting pits and rat pits of England and Ireland and remained unchanged by breeders when the sports were outlawed.

Unrecognized by kennel clubs, the dogs are none-the-less popular and well bred. It is from these animals and the less leggy English Staffordshire Bull Terrier that the American Pit Bull Terrier was bred. They are not heavy dogs, but there is no weight restriction. As one example can look like any ordinary English Staffy, so another can look like any ordinary Pit Bull.

A good dog with its roots firmly in England's Black Country, but preserved by careful breeding in Ireland, buy with care if this is your choice of dog and don't be fooled. Any "Staffy" looking dog without the appropri-

This Staffordshire Bull Terrier was photographed in Ireland by Robert Smith.

ate kennel club registration is not an Irish Staffordshire Bull Terrier. It is a breed in its own right, with its own history.

AMERICAN STAFFORDSHIRE TERRIER

Bigger than the English-bred Staffordshire, and often shown with cropped ears, the American Stafford is, however, still a Stafford. He stands between 17 and 19 inches and weighs up to 50 pounds. Some have called the breed vicious and dangerous, but those who know the breed well claim the opposite is true. Certainly the American Staffordshire Terrier sits as something of a middle ground animal, occupying a place between the Staffordshire Bull Terrier of England and the American Pit Bull Terrier. Being almost a full Pit Bull and almost an English Staffy, yet being neither.

The American Staffordshire Terrier is often shown with cropped ears. Photo by Isabelle Francais.

Although some have called the breed vicious and dangerous, those who know the American Staffordshire Terrier well claim that the opposite is true. Photo by Isabelle Francais.

AMERICAN PIT BULL TERRIER

In recent years throughout Britain and America countless words of abuse have been written about this breed. So much so that it is actually easier in Britain to own a tiger or lion than an American Pit Bull Terrier. One could be forgiven for wondering whether these dogs carry firearms or knives, But no, they do not.

The APBT is a breed in its own right. It is not a mongrel as some kennel clubs maintain and, in the right hands, it is not a dangerous dog, at least no more so than any other powerful breed. Unfortunately, in the wrong hands, like any other powerful dog, the APBT is very dangerous.

These dogs need a great deal of exercise, a firm but even handler and to have their natural exuberance

The American Pit Bull Terrier needs a great deal of exercise. Photo by Isabelle Francais.

The American Pit Bull Terrier stands 18 to 22 inches and weighs anywhere from 30 to 80 pounds. Photo by Isabelle Francais.

capped from time to time. That owners of Pit Bulls need to spend so much time with them working them out and keeping their energy well channeled is an all too often overlooked fact. In size they usually stand 18 to 22 inches and weigh anything from 30 to 80 pounds.

A superb athlete, muscled and powered like few other breeds, the APBT excels at most things. It is highly trainable and desperate to please its owner, but it is not for the beginner or part-time owner.

DOGUE DE BORDEAUX

This dog most definitely belongs in a Bulldog book, perhaps more so than any of the others in its overview of bull-breeds. The Dogue de Bordeaux is the descen-

The head of the Dogue de Bordeaux is massive and obviously of Bulldog origin. Photo by Isabelle Francais.

dent of the Bulldogs taken to Bordeaux by the English kings of earlier times.

It is a big dog, though not a giant, standing between 23 and 27 inches at the shoulder and weighing around 80 to 100 pounds. The head of this dog is massive and obviously of Bulldog origin. It has a great deal of wrinkle to the face and somewhat over-sized paws. Well balanced and strong, the Dogue de Bordeaux is very much like the Bullmastiff, and the similarities between the breeds may explain why the Dogue de Bordeaux never became popular in Britain.

A working, country dog, this breed was used for hunting just about everything that lived in French woods, from bears to wolves, to pigs and boars. Later it became used extensively for cattle droving. Red is its

The Dogue de Bordeaux stands between 23 and 27 inches and weighs around 80 to 100 pounds. Photo by Isabelle Francais.

The Dogo Argentino is a mix of many of the world's finest breeds, including the Bulldog, the Bull Terrier, the Mastiff, the Great Dane, and even the English Pointer. Photo by Isabelle Francais.

usual color. While good with immediate family, it can exhibit aggression to others and thus needs careful control. Having said that, the Dogue de Bordeaux is not bad tempered and is regarded as a good dog with children.

DOGO ARGENTINO (ARGENTINEAN MASTIFF)

This breed is a deliberate and quite recent mix of many of the world's finest breeds.

In the 1920s the Argentinean doctor, Antonio Nores Martinez, set about producing Argentina's first native pure-bred dog. Designed to be able to hunt boar, mountain lion and jaguars moving all day over tough, inhospitable terrain, the Dogo Argentino can call on genes from the Bulldog, the Bull Terrier, the Mastiff,

The Dogo Argentino requires an outdoor life, a strong handler, and good deal of training. Photo by Isabelle Francais.

the Great Dane and even the English Pointer. Quite what the full mix is is anyone's guess, but it stands between 24 and 26 inches tall and weighs up to 95 pounds.

A fine dog that is gaining popularity, the Dogo Argentino requires an outdoor life, a strong handler and a good deal of training. Probably not to be considered by the average town-dwelling family, there is none-the-less room in the wilds for this companion.

PERRO DE PRESA CANARIO

A powerful square-headed dog, with a broad muzzle and slightly raised hindquarters, usually presented with cropped ears, the Perro de Presa Canario is a cross between English Mastiffs and the indigenous, though now extinct, dogs of the Canary Islands. A heavily boned and well muscled dog, the Perro de Presa Canario was bred for dog fighting, stands up to 26 inches tall and weighs up to 110 pounds.

This breed requires a dominant master and a loving family. It is not for beginners and since its demise in the 1960s it has become difficult, if not impossible, to obtain a genuine example of the breed.

It is currently recognized by no authority and would be extinct but for the efforts being made by a few breeders in the Canary Islands and America, whose ongoing attempts to stabilize and consolidate the breed are now beginning to show success.

The Perro de Presa Canario is a cross between Mastiffs and the now extinct dogs of the Canary Islands. Photo by Isabelle Francais.

The Perro de Presa Canario is a powerful square-headed dog with a broad muzzle and is usually presented with cropped ears. Photo by Isabelle Francais.

The Perro de Presa Mallorquin or Mallorquin Bulldog was developed in Spain and Mallorca, in the Balearic Islands, for baiting and dog fighting. Today, it is almost extinct, and the dogs that do exist are mostly companion dogs. Photo by Isabelle Francais.

PERRO DE PRESA MALLORQUIN (MALLORQUIN BULLDOG)

The sport of bull baiting was always popular in Spain, and Mallorca, in the Balearic Islands, developed this dog for baiting and dog fighting. It is a formidable animal with a broad Bulldog chest and near Mastiff height. It should not exceed 80 pounds in weight and stands 23 inches tall. There is some historic evidence to support the theory that the foundation of the breed is made up of Mastiff, Bulldog and local indigenous breeds, though the exact make up is, and probably always will be, unknown.

Whether one can obtain an example of this breed is questionable. Even in Mallorca the locals claim the breed has now been crossed out from its original state, and while a number still exists, these are mostly companion dogs. They are almost extinct, but if one is secured, be sure to discipline it well from puppyhood.

Lana's "Van Shelton" Lane is the double grandson of Lana's "Marcelle" Lane, the foundations sire of Alapaha Blue Blood Bulldogs. Owner Lana Lou Lane.

ALAPAHA BLUE BLOOD BULLDOG

Though not a well-known breed, the growing popularity of the Alapaha makes its inclusion in our book necessary. This might be called a "natural" Bulldog, although deliberate breeding and design played an important part in its development.

In Rebecca, Georgia, a long-term breeding program continued today by Lana Lou Lane was set up to save the plantation dog of southern Georgia. Through generations of crossing in Bulldog stock the mix was stabilized and today a remarkable, if somewhat localized, dog is the result of Papa Buck Lane's dream all those years ago.

The Alapaha is a powerful working hunting dog that weighs up to 100 pounds and stands 24 inches at the shoulder. The females are noticeably smaller, but no less active. Ears and tail are never docked and the body is powerful, set on powerful, but clumsy legs. The head is well shaped but the bite and undershot mouth is not over emphasized. It is said by owners of this dog that it needs little control and is a sweet-natured family companion. It is more than a match for any game that threaten its charges and is easily and quickly trained.

No organization currently recognizes the breed, but that said, this breed will surely increase in popularity as time passes. While we may not see one in showrings for many, many years to come, we may well see them on some farms. They are and will remain a specialty working dog.

BOXER

As a member of the bull-breed family, the Boxer must rank almost with the Bulldog itself and is a fitting breed to finish our book off with. The Boxer is more refined than many other bull-breeds, and more lithe, but a good well-built Boxer can almost look like and weigh the same as a Bulldog of the "Crib" and "Rosa" era (1820s). It might be said that the Boxer is the German Bulldog, but without doubt it was the infusion of genes from the British Bulldog that lends the Boxer its bull-quality. While the German "bullenbeiser" was the foundation dog, the first dog in the German Boxer Stud Book is "Flocki," the son of a white British Bulldog. "Flocki" was born in 1895 and was the first Boxer ever to be shown.

However, if the genetic make up of the Boxer includes a big part of British Bulldog, the preservation of the breeds health and well being is due entirely to the expertise and skill, caring and forethought of the German Boxer breeders. When the trendsetters in

The Boxer is more refined than other bull-breeds. It might be said that the Boxer is the German Bulldog. Photo by Isabelle Francais.

Britain went in search of fashionable extremes, the Germans kept an eye constantly on function.

The Boxer, like all good bull-breed dogs, is stable, good natured and fearless. It is an active dog with good breathing and high intelligence. It stands up to 25 inches and weighs in at up to 70 pounds. Of course, these are guidelines only, and Boxers come in many sizes, from lithe springy lightweights to real heavy-weights. The Boxer though should never be too heavy to move properly.

While a predominantly white coat is a disqualification in the show ring, the true bull-breed enthusiast and true Boxer lover should not let such trivial matters interfere with their choice. A white Boxer is a Boxer— full stop.

Epilogue

History should always be recorded, by as many people as possible, before times past become times forgotten. The speed of change sometimes only manifests itself when we recall, with words and pictures, what went before. And we must look closely, we must genuinely try to see what we are looking at and not just look at what we want to see.

Times and tastes change, but change and improvement are not always the same thing. We are not to know, caught up as we are in the momentum of social change, whether what we are developing and what we are allowing to alter is going to prove beneficial or not. We cannot be blamed for embarking on the wrong road if the road has never been trod before...but we are guilty of ignorance and arrogance if, seeing that we have taken the wrong path, we pretend that we cannot right the mistakes we have made.

To admit, after a long journey, that we have arrived at the wrong albeit comfortable destination is difficult; to leave that comfortable place and go back takes great courage and fortitude. To admit that the journey wasn't wise, or even necessary, takes even greater courage and a good deal of honesty. Not everyone wants to make such admissions and not everyone will make the journey back. That is their choice but they must not try to stop those who are willing.

Therein lies the essence of all genuine progress. If an experiment, however long, does not work out, the beginning must be returned to and the work begun again.

Index